RESPOND, VOLUME 3

RESPOND

VOLUME 3

A RESOURCE BOOK
FOR YOUTH MINISTRY

Edited by MASON L. BROWN

JUDSON PRESS, Valley Forge

RESPOND, VOLUME 3

Library of Congress Cataloging in Publication Data
Main entry under title:
Respond; a resource book for youth ministry.
    Vol. 2 edited by J. M. Corbett; v. 3 by M. L. Brown.
    Includes bibliographies.
    1. Religious education—Text-books for young people—
Baptist. I. Ignatius, Keith L., ed. II. Corbett, Janice M.,
ed. III. Brown, Mason L., ed.
BX6225.R47   268′.4   77-159050
ISBN 0-8170-0600-1 (v. 3)

Printed in the U.S.A.

Photo credits: cover and p. 34, Heinz Fussle; p. 49, Richard
McPhee; p. 67, Wallowitch; p. 91, Bob Combs; p. 113, Rohn Engh.

What do I as an adult have to offer youth?
  My whole self. All that I am and feel as a person.
  The built-in maturity and love I have found in the midst of life,
    which I can share.
  Given not by the truckload but like daily vitamin pills.

What do I as an adult have to offer youth?
  The opportunity to plan together and carry out significant
    group experiences with the church.
  Experiences which we can look forward to with hope and expectancy
    and look back upon with meaning and joy.

What do I as an adult have to offer youth?
  Freedom which they can handle.
  Limits where they are needed.
  Limits that are clarified and enforced with love, consistency,
    and forgiveness.
  Some of my wealth, being not a briber nor a skinflint.
  All of my friendship, my love, my faith in God as known in
    Jesus Christ and as biblically revealed.
  Separation from adults, to be alone or with youth friends
    when needed.
  Hope when they are discouraged.
  Meaning when life has fallen apart.
  And a laugh now and then to break tension and
    develop oneness across our age differences.

That is what I as an adult have to offer youth.

Mason L. Brown

Pick it up!
     Hold it!
          Love it!
          See it as a beautiful example of a youth ministry resource and then—

We Suggest You Do This!

Browse through the book to see what's hidden behind its innocent look. Note the various sections. Read a couple of the plans. Get a feel of what's here and what may have some possibilities for your group. Discover the sensation of gripping an extensive compilation of action and study resources and leadership helps that have never been produced before. Realize, however, that—

It's Not the Gospel.

Respond is a book of suggestions. Don't be afraid to modify, tear out, change, or discard any of the material that is of no value to your group. (The editor will never know.) But don't throw away some stuff that you may use later—like twelve months from now.

Stay with It!

Browse through the book several times. Get to know it inside out. And when the moment comes that your group has an idea it wants to explore, but no resources, you can say, "Hey, I've got just the thing!" Flip to the appropriate page and surprise the "living daylights" out of them.

When Using the Suggested Articles:

1. *Read* through the session plans in order to get an idea of what the session is about.
2. *Reread* the target or purpose. Restate it in your own words. Then ask: Does it fit the group? How should it be changed? What other appropriate experiences does it enable you to recall?
3. *Reread* the procedures. How do they fit the needs of your group—size, temperament, amount of session time, setting, room size, equipment, leadership, etc.?
4. *Recheck* the preparation which will be needed. Do you have enough time to get ready for the session? Necessary resources? Leadership?
5. If you've got the answer to all those questions, get on with it and have a successful experience.

ONE FINAL COMMENT

Respond took a lot of hard work by a lot of people to produce. Our reasons for doing the book are:
1. It will make your work in youth ministry a little easier;
2. it will make you smile
     more often
     and not worry so much
     about where you are in youth
     ministry;
3. it will help your group and the gospel get together
     more often and more intimately.

Good luck,
Good reading, and
A great ministry!

> —From the people
> of *Respond*

A NOTE ABOUT RESPOND, VOLUME 3

Respond 3, like *Respond 1* and *2* before it, incorporates the practical advice, down-to-earth ideas, and "meaty" study suggestions helpful in youth ministry. An index to *Respond,* volumes 1, 2, and 3, is provided at the back of the book. If you have a study topic in mind and need resources, check the index.

In some of the suggestions to the leader, use of a copy machine for advance preparation is one of the options. There is probably someone in your church who has access to a copy machine at a cost that is not prohibitive. You have permission to make extra copies of this material which would actually be used by your local church youth group.

CONTENTS

Section 1
RESOURCES FOR STUDY AND ACTION

Exploring the Word of God
Easter
Ecology
Evangelism
Christian Faith
Meditation
International Mission
Meeting Personal Needs
The Christian and the Community
Sexuality
Vocation
Literature and Faith
Feelings and Faith

CREATIVE BIBLICAL STUDY
by ROBERT F. WALK II

INTRODUCTION

Assuming that God's relationship to persons is creative and purposeful, how then can we turn to the text of the Bible and wrestle with it creatively? In the context of ministering with youth, use of the Bible becomes an area of crucial concern. How can we approach the source book of the Christian faith creatively, in such a way that its concerns will come alive? The Bible was the product of people walking the many roads of life and encountering the living God amidst the eternal issues of life and death. The Bible became, with God's help, a record of those personal experiences in words and with the feeling of faith. Taking a cue from the way the Bible was written we can approach the study of the Bible creatively.

PLANS

The first possibility is a group session on "Record Sounds and the Bible." One of the powerful forces which youth face is mass media. We all are bombarded with a continual flow of sights, sounds, and vibrations. Begin with the sounds of music. Study the themes of records as they relate to the themes of the Bible. Ask the group members to bring their favorite records or tape recordings. Then develop the session through the following steps:

1. Have a listening period—listen to the lyrics as well as to the music. Listen to the words, feelings, and themes presented.
2. Retain the thoughts and feelings of the record by listing them on newsprint, expressing them through a collage, the use of clay, or painting.
3. Have the group search the Scriptures for themes related to those of the records. For example, if the theme was "love," study 1 Corinthians 13.
4. Compare love as presented in the record and as it comes across in the Bible. Bible com-

mentaries and a concordance will help in locating biblical themes. Alternate listening to a particular record with reading the biblical record.

A creative means of communicating the insights and learnings of records and the Bible might be a mass media approach. Divide responsibilities among group members. Have part of your group work on a self-styled 8mm movie that would capture the themes of both the Bible and the record. Check around. Someone in the church membership probably owns an 8mm camera which they will lend your group.

Another group could work on the script. As sound for the movie, tape the music of the records on one recorder and the words of Scripture on another. The simultaneous combination of messages ought to make more meaningful the truths of the Bible as they intersect with the concerns of life.

A second approach could be a group session on "Advertising Vibrations and the Bible." Another media force that penetrates young people deeply is the blurbs of the advertising industry. Have a creative Bible study on the themes of the Bible and the themes of advertising. An approach for developing the session might look like this:

1. Begin by having the young people cut ads out of newspapers and magazines. Paste these on newsprint.
2. Also urge the group to brainstorm about ads they remember from television and radio. Record these on newsprint or a chalkboard.
3. Have the group examine what the ads are saying, asking questions such as:
   * What do the ads say about people?
   * What do they reveal about human relationships?
   * Why are pretty girls used to sell so many products?
   * Does success in life really depend upon using a certain product?

13

- How do ads tend to control our minds and wills?
- What are the purposes of advertising?

4. Now have the group or groups open the Bible and wrestle with what it says about people, human relationships, and success in life. Utilize the following passages in your search:

Bibles Needed

- *Psalm 8*—To stimulate thinking about the purpose and meaning of man.
- *Matthew 25:31-46*—Ads sometimes give the impression you are not "in" and "accepted" unless you use the "right" product. What does the Scripture say about acceptance and human relationships?
- *Luke 12:22-31*—What does this say about our values and priorities? What ought they to be? How does our thirst for material possessions affect our life values?
- *Matthew 4:1-11*—What issues did Jesus struggle with in the temptations? Power? Wealth? Material versus spiritual? In what ways do ads tempt us with similar issues? How can we learn to be in charge of our minds and decisions?

A creative follow-up to the learning of this session might be to have the youth write up spot commercials on the meaning of God, faith, man, values, success, etc. These could be taped, written down, acted out in skit form, or painted on posters. The tapes or skits could be used as part of a church worship service. They could be shared with another age group or class during church school. Posters could be hung in church vestibules and/or maybe some store windows in town. In some areas the councils of churches are sponsoring spot commercials on radio. Maybe your group could explore the idea. The means and techniques of adver-

tising can be used to give greater depth to the meaning of life and to being human in the image of God.

A third method of creative Bible study is INNER LIFE FORCES AND THE BIBLE. This is not so much a group endeavor as an ongoing personal approach. As well as outside influences on the life-style and faith of young people, there are inner forces. With these in mind, encourage individuals in your group to begin keeping a daily or weekly written record of their personal activities, thoughts, feelings, dreams, hopes, disappointments, problems, relationships, and whatever else they feel is important to them. Relate these life experiences to the personal histories of such personalities as Abraham, Moses, Joseph, Ruth, Job, Isaiah, Jeremiah, Jesus, and Paul. As we read these personal histories in the Bible, we should keep in mind the following questions and relate them to our own lives:

- What were the main events of the lives of these biblical personalities?
- What were their strengths? Weaknesses?
- With what questions did they struggle?
- What part did faith in God play in their lives?
- What were their life goals?

In the light of these reflections we should be able to zero in more closely on where we are going in life and how to get there. Some group sessions could be based on the issues arising from these findings. Such a diary of life and Bible concerns is a means of shaping our growing life and faith.

The Word of God is creative. God's written word, the Bible, becomes the creative living Word in young people and adults as they are open and responsive to the leading of God's Spirit in their lives. In Christ the Word became flesh. May these approaches to life and the Bible cause the Word to become flesh in you, furthering your personal and group experiences in the abundant life.

HE TOLD THEM PARABLES

by CHARLES R. LANDON, JR.

TARGET

To understand the parable as a literary form and as a teaching tool and to study in depth one of Jesus' parables.

ADVANCE PLANNING

1. At your meeting immediately preceding this session, assign to members of your group the task of obtaining definitions (from dictionaries or grammar books) of these literary forms: allegory, parable, simile, analogy, riddle, metaphor, fable, myth, proverb.
2. Write each of the above literary form names on a separate piece of paper and tape the papers to the wall of your meeting place. When the definitions are given at the beginning of the session, have someone write them with magic markers on the appropriate papers.
3. Obtain from your pastor, church, community library, or some other source some commentaries on the Gospels or some one-volume Bible commentaries. Some suggestions: William Barclay's *Daily Study Bible,* the *Abingdon Bible Commentary,* the *New Bible Commentary Revised,* the *Wycliffe Bible Commentary.* Since these will be used for background information rather than for interpretation, you will not need technical commentaries nor older devotional books.

Advance preparation is needed here

INTRODUCTION

The first three Gospels—Matthew, Mark, and Luke—devote considerable space to Jesus' most familiar form of teaching, his parables. There are about thirty-five of these parables. Though they appear simple and straightforward, their interpretation and understanding has been a major subject for debate among Bible scholars throughout the history of Christianity.

Biblical parables have been simplistically defined as "earthly stories with heavenly meanings," but this description belies their complexity. It also camouflages the sensationalism that has characterized much parable commentary through the centuries. In more recent years, Bible scholars have developed a set of guidelines to facilitate and standardize the interpretation and understanding of Jesus' parables.

Four of these guidelines are:
1. Each parable must be viewed from the perspective of the life situation in which it was told. Thus we must learn as much as we can about Palestinian Jewish customs and environment, since these factors constituted the life situation of Jesus' parables.
2. Generally speaking, each parable is designed to teach one central truth, though there may also be secondary teachings. The details of the parable are meant to reinforce this central truth, rather than to be interpreted individually or literally.
3. When Jesus provides introductory or explanatory remarks with the parable, the parable must be understood within the context of these remarks. The parable of the sower (Matthew 13:3-23) is an example of a parable with an explanation.
4. Each parable must also be understood within the context of the passage in which it is located.

For example, the parable of the good Samaritan (Luke 10:30-37) was told by Jesus in response to a lawyer's testing question.

This session will attempt to define and identify the parable as a literary form and then see how Jesus used one parable in his teaching.

PLANS

1. LITERARY FORMS

Have the people who researched the definitions of various literary forms write their definitions with magic markers on the appropriate papers taped on the walls. Note the distinctive nature of a parable. Share with the group, as informally as possible, the material on parables in the "Introduction" to this session. Then, on a chalkboard or large piece of newsprint, list as many of the parables as the group can name.

2. RESEARCH

Divide the group into three smaller groups. Each will study the parable of the mustard seed: Group 1 will study Matthew 13:31-32; Group 2, Mark 4:30-32; and Group 3, Luke 13:18-19. Allow members of each group to select copies of the commentaries you have collected to assist them. Then have each group answer these questions about this parable (make enough copies of this list for each group to have one):

• What is unique about the mustard seed/plant?
• Why would Jesus select this particular seed/ plant for his parable?
• Is there some special meaning to the birds? To the branches? To the nests?

• What is meant by the "kingdom of Heaven"?
• What do you think is the central truth/teaching of this parable?

3. DISCUSSION

Have the groups reassemble into one group and compare answers to the questions. There will probably be general agreement that the central truth/teaching of the parable is that of growth of the kingdom of God, from tiny beginnings to vastness. To illustrate that this growth has indeed occurred, conclude the program with one or more of these activities:

a. Look at the beginnings of several of Paul's letters which suggest that the kingdom of God was spreading widely even in Paul's time. Compare Romans 1:8, Colossians 1:6, and 1 Thessalonians 1:8 to the tiny band of terrified disciples hiding in their "upper room" after the crucifixion of Christ.

b. Using a map of the world, illustrate the spread of the kingdom into all the world. Other resources include the various newsmagazines, denominational magazines, and other publications which carry reports of the "younger churches," such as Thailand or Zaire.

c. Read through with your group the words of the hymn "Jesus Shall Reign," which is a joyous affirmation of the truth of this parable.

d. Share a time of prayer, praising and thanking God for the extension of his Good News into all the world.

16

BRINGING THE PARABLES ALIVE
by CHARLES R. LANDON, JR.

TARGET

To sharpen our ability to understand biblical parables, especially their relevance to contemporary life.

PLANNING

1. Have on hand the commentaries, as well as several different translations and paraphrases of the New Testament.

2. Try to read for yourself before the session Helmut Thielicke's two sermons on the "Parable of the Prodigal Son" in his book *The Waiting Father: Sermons on the Parables of Jesus* (New York: Harper & Row, Publishers, 1959).
3. If you used the program "He Told Them Parables," reflect on what happened in the group and in you during and as a result of this program.

INTRODUCTION

The two most familiar biblical parables, even to those who are otherwise biblically illiterate, are the parable of the good Samaritan (Luke 10:30-37), and the parable of the prodigal son (Luke 15:11-32). The latter has been the text for countless sermons to youth, normally with an emphasis on the folly of the younger son's ways and an exhortation to return to the Father and live as one should. But is this really what Jesus was trying to illustrate; is this the central truth/teaching of this parable? Helmut Thielicke calls this the "Parable of the Prodigal Son." Other commentators have called it the "Parable of the Lost Son," since it is presented by Luke along with the parables of the lost sheep and the lost coin. This session is an attempt to understand this parable and then to translate it into contemporary terms.

PLANS

1. REVIEW

Go over with the group the first session's materials on parables in general, reiterating the four guidelines for interpretation and understanding. It would be wise to list these in abbreviated form on newsprint and tape to the wall as a visible reminder. An abbreviated form might be:
• Life situation
• One central teaching
• Jesus' remarks
• Bible context.

2. RESEARCH

Break the group into three or four small groups and have each of them use a different translation or paraphrase of the New Testament to study the passage (Luke 15:11-32) and then answer these questions (make enough copies of these questions for each group to have a copy and supply the groups with newsprint sheets and felt-tip pens to jot down their thoughts):
• What is the life situation pictured in this parable?

• Who are the primary characters? Secondary?
• Who do you think is the main character?
• With which of the characters do you identify most strongly or readily?
• What do you think is the central truth/teaching of this parable?

3. DISCUSSION

Reassemble the group and discuss the answers and opinions that have developed. It is important that you foster an atmosphere of openness rather than correctness, particularly as pertaining to identification with the characters. If you have not overdone this method in other programs, role-play the parable, assigning one person to each role. Or group role-play it with each character in the parable portrayed collectively by a small group. Allow time to discuss the feelings and dynamics that develop.

4. CREATIVE ACTIVITY

Have each person create a parable which communicates in modern terms what he believes to be the central truth/teaching of this parable. Or have small groups of two to four persons create such parables. Allow time for sharing the creations and for discussion. Be sure no one is put down or rejected through ridicule.

5. CLOSING WORSHIP

Read through the words of the hymn "There's a Wideness in God's Mercy," and share a time of quiet thanks to God for his mercy to us.

A Lenten-Easter program on the meaning of the crucifixion-resurrection event

Plan ahead for this program. Film "The Red Balloon" must be reserved ahead of time.

UP, UP, AND AWAY!

by ROBERT A. NOBLETT

GETTING STARTED

At the outset of any conversation about the crucifixion-resurrection event in the life of Jesus Christ, there is a danger to be noted—the danger of being obsessed with mechanics to the exclusion of meanings. The community of faith should be concerned with the implications of the event for present existence.

If the resurrection had not occurred, there would be no Christian church. The story of the early church (Acts) and its subsequent development is ample testimony to the reality of the resurrection. This is the theme that Paul sounds in his first letter to the Corinthian Christians: "If there be no resurrection, then Christ was not raised; and if Christ was not raised, then our gospel is null and void, and so is your faith; and we turn out to be lying witnesses for God, because we bore witness that he raised Christ to life, whereas, if the dead are not raised, he did not raise him" (1 Corinthians 15:13-15, NEB). Think of the matter in these terms: I do not have to have a detailed understanding of aeronautics in order to allow a jet to carry me from Boston to Los Angeles; its power is of great service to me, even if I am a mechanical idiot! So also the resurrection. In order to be lifted by it, we need not know its metaphysics.

To break open a conversation about the crucifixion-resurrection event, the group should become familiar with the biblical material which reveals it. This goal can be accomplished by dividing into groups of four persons and having each group read one of the Gospel records regarding the trial-crucifixion-resurrection (Matthew 27–28:20; Mark 14:53–16:8; Luke 22:54–24; John 18:12–20:25). Following this, while still in small groups, ask for the various feeling responses the participants had while they read the material (or heard it read for them). Jot these responses down on a piece of newsprint. Share these feelings with the total group.

GETTING INTO IT

In order to understand fully the meaning of the crucifixion, it is important that we give it meaning in terms of present-day behavior. Ask the group to study the meanings of the word "crucifixion." Of course we do not hear of crucifixions in the sense of someone being nailed to a piece of wood, but we do nonetheless see evidence of crucifixion. The Random House Dictionary suggests as its last definition of crucify "to treat with gross injustice; persecute." That suggests some new ways in which to think of it. We can crucify people by spreading rumors about them, by denying them the staples of existence (food, financial well-being, etc.), by treating them unfairly, or merely by being indifferent to them. Have the participants relate contemporary examples of crucifixion in their families, their schools, their community, or the larger world.

Do likewise with the theme of resurrection. Ask the participants to give evidence of resurrection in everyday, common events. For example springtime, recovery from illness, reconciliation between people, and a new self-image, are all events which resemble the resurrection. Again turning to the Random House Dictionary, remind them that apart from the particular event we call "the resurrection," the word means "a rising again, as from decay, or disuse, etc.; revival."

1. THE HEART OF THE MATTER

But why does one willingly participate in self-giving even to the extent of death? Why does a soldier fling himself atop a grenade and save his comrades from destruction at the cost of his own life? Why would a parent quickly lay down his or her life for that of a son or daughter? Why did Jesus Christ tolerate the cross when he could have changed courses and lived? Though the word is overworked and often therefore trite, love is the answer to these questions. We give of ourselves when we feel the object of our affection is indeed worthy of the sacrifice, is in fact dear enough to call forth such self-surrender. This is the biblical affirmation about God and us: "For God is love; and his love was disclosed to us in this, that he sent his only Son into the world to bring us life. The love I speak of is not our love for God, but the love he showed to us in sending his Son as the remedy for the defilement of our sins" (1 John 4:9-11, NEB). Furthermore, crucifixion—either our own or another's—is often the matrix out of which resurrection comes. When I enter into the misery of another, there is new life for both of us. When I am able to face my sickness, I have taken the first step in the recovery of health.

Have the group talk about motives for self-sacrifice and the results of such an action. Ask them to think of people they have known who have done this and what it led to. Ask them about occasions when they have seen something close to a crucifixion and have been moved to compassion, thereby experiencing something close to a resurrection. Or when they have been crucified, have forgiven, and have experienced resurrection.

2. FEELING THE MATTER

To communicate the idea of crucifixion-resurrection, you can portray it graphically and dramatically. One of the most effective ways in which this theme can be felt is to view a short, color film entitled *The Red Balloon*. This film is the story of a young boy in Paris who makes friends with a red balloon and his subsequent adventure in keeping the balloon safe from destruction. The absence of dialogue, coupled with the fact that the film has been widely acclaimed for its effectiveness, is ample evidence that the acting is superb. By means of music, body movement, and facial expres-

sion, the themes of suffering, crucifixion, and resurrection are richly and meaningfully presented. Check with local film libraries about its rental or with Brandon Films, Inc. (221 West 57th St., New York, N.Y. 10019). The film lasts 34 minutes.

Following its presentation, invite the group's response, especially in regard to the essence of resurrection. What does it mean to be resurrected NOW? When the Bible speaks of eternal life, it speaks of eternal life that can be realized at the present moment. The theme of our program is "Up, Up, and Away," and what we are suggesting is that the Christian person is one who realizes that he/she is free to participate in the spirit of Christ's resurrection and lives pro-life; he or she is free to develop to the utmost of his God-given potential. "Praise be to the God and Father of our Lord Jesus Christ, who in his great mercy gave us new birth into a living hope by the resurrection of Jesus Christ from the dead!" (1 Peter 1:3, NEB).

A feeling for resurrection could also be experienced by listening to the song "To Life" from the Broadway musical *Fiddler on the Roof*. The same follow-up would be encouraged.

3. COMING TO A CLOSE

To further the group's understanding of resurrection, try giving it tangible expression. If *The Red Balloon* is shown, distribute balloons, inflate them, and invite the group to put meaningful symbols on them with magic markers, and then bat them about. Perhaps someone in the group dances and could perform a dance that would be suggestive of new life, or the group could make collages that would present vibrancy and hope.

In any event, the program will be most useful when each one present is enabled to feel the power of resurrection.

RECYCLING: A PERSONAL REVOLUTION
by DAPHNE GILLISPIE

TARGET

To become more sensitive to what makes waste and to discover where the individual can help diminish that waste.

INTRODUCTION

How can one approach the question of ecology's destiny? Long after industry and government have drawn up plans to correct our wayward waste of resources, the individual still must act to correct these wasteful trends. So let us examine what the individual can do rather than sit back and wait for industry or government to do our "dirty" work for us.

PREPARATION

Supplies Needed

The person in charge of the meeting should gather together "disposables." (The term "disposa-ables" is misleading because it implies that plastic items can in fact be disposed of; on the contrary, most of these so-called "disposables" are not bio-degradable and therefore are not disposed of at all. In other words, they do not decompose and break down into components that can reenter the natural cycle. Instead, these materials clog and clutter, forming permanent monuments to man's mindless wastefulness.)

The person in charge should place these "dis-posables" (plastic spoons, bottles, x-ray paper, pill containers, etc.) in the center of the room—enough should be brought for at least one per person expected. Any posters or flyers that can be collected or created can be hung on the walls.

21

PROCEDURE

1. USING DISPOSABLES

Each person should pick one of the items from the center of the room and should ponder possible uses for this item. Enough time should be allowed for creative and earnest thought. Try to think beyond the obvious or common suggestion.

After each person has had a chance to think through his item's uses and perhaps has recorded them, he should report to the total group, while a recorder records the suggestions on a flip chart or chalkboard. (Answers may range from household uses to art and craft possibilities. An interesting aside here is that a camp in New Hampshire is doing all of its arts and crafts from recycled items.)

When the suggestions are all listed, they should be sorted generally into categories of commonality: household, office, arts and crafts, etc. Divide the group into task forces by category for about fifteen or twenty minutes to discuss ways of implementing some of the ideas suggested. For example, if a person has picked a plastic pill container for his item and knows how to make a medallion by melting it in a hot oven, he might suggest that the church collect these for a camp project or for some other purpose.

Recycling can bring renewal in relationships. Also programs should instruct or enable a person to do something with the information learned. From this session your group might outline projects for the remainder of the year, involving many people outside your youth group as well.

2. REFLECTION

After a brainstorming session, spend some time reflecting upon what has happened. Some questions to help focus this pondering are these:

- What personal changes am I willing to make regarding recycling and consumption?
- How can I influence others to do some of the same? (The personal revolution involves you, but witnessing includes others.)
- What conclusions can be drawn from our emphasis on "throw-awayism"? (Specifically, what value is placed upon something that is created to be thrown away?)
- What more lofty achievements might man create so that his creations might be lasting "things of beauty"?

3. PONDER

Perhaps someone could read Psalm 84 aloud.

4. PRAYER

Help us, O God, to love and respect you and your creation enough to preserve it for posterity. We regret that our nation encourages "throw-awayism." We are tantalized by paper towels, plastic cups and spoons. We are encouraged to be efficient, get it done. Eat and dispose, clean and dispose. Save us from this false sense of efficiency and from our own ignorances. Restore to each of us a keen sense of responsibility for what we do and how we do it. Amen.

CHRISTIAN WITNESS

by RICHARD D. ORR

TARGET

To explore styles of witnessing in today's world.

INTRODUCTION

Is your life a true reflection of your faith? "Only let your manner of life be worthy of the gospel of Christ" (Philippians 1:27). *Every* Christian is a priest and prophet, a disciple, one who proclaims the Good News of God's love for all people. The teachings of Jesus are filled with instructions about sharing with the poor, about being concerned with the directions of society, about confronting the misuse of political or economic or religious power, about the need for justice and good relations.

Jesus' teachings are also filled with suggestions about an inner change and newness that exhibits itself in a self-awareness and appreciation, an "I-ness" that is deep enough and sure enough to invite the deepest, most "headed-toward-wholeness" self from other persons. "Love your neighbor as yourself" (Matthew 22:39) means paying attention to, remembering, discovering who *you* are and what *your* human situation means and also responding with sincere paying-attention and remembering and discovering about your fellowman. What is telling the "Good News"? What is the shape of the "invitation to wholeness"? How does one "share Christ"? Let's do some exploring together.

SESSION OPTIONS

1. ROLE-PLAYING

The situation is one in which four friends are gathered together for a reunion. These friends have been high school classmates and have since gone on to school or work and become adult members of the local church. Three of the persons, Penny, Ben, and Will, have continued in their hometown and in the same church. Rick left the old hometown and went off to find his vocation and values in a city faraway. Rick is home for vacation and is at a gathering with Penny, Ben, and Will. All of these three have particular ideas about what is most important to tell about their church and their faith.

In an initial conversation, let them each try to convince Rick that he should be involved in the church for the reason that each one holds as having the most importance. Some of the possible role ideas are:

PENNY loves the choir, the music, and the general feeling of "awe" that she gets from the worship service. She seeks to convince Rick that this is something that is missing from his life and that he ought to have.

BEN is very convinced that the educational mission of the church is at the heart of the Christian faith. He tells Rick of the "new models" they are developing in their church school and adult classes. He tries to convince Rick that he ought to be involved in this investigation and pilgrimage.

WILL is very enamored with the church as an institution in society and in particular its building. He tries to convince Rick that the church building has made a substantial contribution to the outreach of God in the community and that Rick ought to be involved with an institution that is making this contribution.

Step 1: The initial conversation in which each of the participants tries to "convince" Rick.

Step 2: Let each of the three (Penny, Ben, and Will) go back to a smaller group of participants and let this group tell their "star" in the role play what he/she should have said and how to proceed in the next conversation.

Step 3: A second conversation between the role players, in which Penny, Ben, and Will act on the instructions of their small group.

Step 4: Discuss what happened and the ideas that were brought to light. How did you feel about these ideas? How did they relate to the content of the Christian witness?

2. TELLING WHAT'S HAPPENED TO YOU

One possible definition of Christian witness is to tell your story, to tell those things that have meaning to you, those events that have revealed direction to you, and those beliefs that are most important to your understanding of how human lives interact with God's plan and Jesus' presence. The idea is that you can't speak for anyone else or you can't judge anyone else's story, but you can always tell what's happened to you as clearly and with as much concreteness as possible.

Step 1: Give everyone a large piece of newsprint and a felt pen or crayon.

Step 2: Ask each person to write the things that he honestly could say in telling what's happened to his/her life to influence understanding. One way to approach this might be to ask the members to break up these statements into categories:

- What are two or three of the things that you can honestly say you deeply believe with no hesitation, or how would you say the things you believe?
- What are two or three of the events in your life that have helped to shape it in the way that it is going?

- What do you see as being at the *heart* of the Christian message that you could tell about, based upon your experience and "what has happened to you"?

Step 3: Let each person share his or her witness in as direct and succinct a way as possible. Remember, this is not speaking for anyone else or implying that anyone else ought to have the same experience or the same beliefs as you. This is telling what has happened to you.

3. EXPLORING DIRECTIONS FROM THE BIBLE

Step 1: Assign each of the following texts to a person or a small group of persons for exploration:

Mark 10:17-22, The rich young man

Luke 19:1-10, The tax collector, Zacchaeus

Luke 7:36-50, The woman who was a sinner

Matthew 6:1-6, How to practice piety

Luke 18:9-14, The Pharisee and the publican

Luke 4:16-21, Instructions from Isaiah

Luke 10:29-37, A style of caring

Matthew 10:5-15, Sending out the Twelve

Matthew 5:20-26, Jesus and the law

Matthew 8:18-22, Witnessing and excuses

Step 2: Let the small group or person decide what has happened in the situation in the text. Identify as clearly as possible the setting and happening and who is seeking instruction about witnessing. What is the type and style of witnessing that is presented in the story or instruction? How would you put the instructions about witnessing that are presented here into your own words? Try to isolate two or three guidelines about Christian witness which seem to come from this text which you would be able to understand as instructions for you in this time.

Step 3: Let the individuals or groups share their understanding of the text and the guidelines they have discovered. Make a composite list on the chalkboard or newsprint of the guidelines emerging and discuss them together.

4. REFLECTING ABOUT WITNESS

Step 1: Place each of the following short sentences at the top of a piece of large newsprint around the room where you have your meeting. A copy machine would help with this preparation task.

Step 2: Let the persons who are participating walk around the room in ones or twos and make some reflective reaction to the statement they read at the top of the sheet.

Step 3: Ask them to put their remarks, comments, reactions, observations, and feelings in the blank space left on the newsprint sheet.

Step 4: Discuss the statements together with the reactions and try to come to some group consensus about which ideas seem to fit best with their feelings and beliefs.

Statements are as follows:

• The real battles of faith today are being fought in factories, shops, offices, farms, political parties, government agencies, in homes, in the press, and in the relationship of nations. The church should go into these spheres to work for the coming of the kingdom.

• The way Christians in the church ought to work at revealing God's love for the world is by regularly *planning opportunities* for praise and celebration of God's creation and the gifts he has given us.

• In a world that is torn by the divisions of generation differences, by the divisions of races, and by the divisions of countries at war, the primary witness of the Christian faith must be to work for understanding, for brotherhood, and the deepest of reconciliation.

• The major focus of the Christian message is a man's soul and his personal assurance that he is a citizen of heaven and one of God's chosen witnesses.

• In Christian witness, the appeal ought to be to the person's feelings and his understanding of letting Christ into his heart and not to his intellect or his work.

• Christ calls us, as members of the church, to be the leaven that leavens the world and the salt of the earth. Are we to accomplish this task by working with the major institutions of society or by working with individual persons and their goals?

- As Christian witnesses we have a product and we are called to sell it.
- Even when persons are not aware of their need, we have a responsibility to share our testimony and the Good News that we have experienced.
- The Christian witness is telling what's happened to you.
- The Christian testimony has to be a word of reassurance and answers.

5. EXPLORING DIRECTIONS

Divide the participants into three task groups and give them the following materials to work on for fifteen to twenty minutes. Again a copy machine will help with preparation.

Step 1: *Task Group #1*—With the material we have already investigated, through the Bible, the statements, and our own sharing of experiences, define together and make a list of some of the best ways that we, in this particular place and given the persons we are, might be able to give *personal individual* witness to our faith and experiences.

Task Group #2—With the material we have already discussed, decide and make a list of some of the best ways that we, in this place and given the persons that we are, might be able to *act as a group* or act within the groups and institutions already present in our community in a style of witnessing that is consistent with the instructions of the Bible and our understanding of the Christian faith.

Task Group #3—With the things we have already discussed, decide and

make a list of the best ways that we will be able to suggest that *our church* may be able to enhance its style of witness and outreach.

Step 2: Discuss these various options together and decide which ones have major priority and begin making some assignments and time definitions about when we will start acting on them individually and together.

6. A MOMENT OF CELEBRATION AND DEDICATION

Step 1: Begin the celebration with the singing of songs that have special meaning to the group.

Step 2: Have readers read two or three of the texts that have been investigated in the earlier part of the sharing.

Step 3: A Litany of Intention: Invite as many persons as would like to do so to share their feelings in the following formula: "Because God is _____, (e.g., kind, inviting, loving, etc.). I will try to be _____ (your intentions).

Step 4: A Gathering of Voices for Closing: Let the leader say a phrase and the community repeat it in similar mood:

The time is alive for telling Good News.
Our lives can be messages.
Our minds can bring the gift of reason.
Our imaginations can be festive freshness.
Our spirits can sense needs.
Let strength come.
Let meaning be experienced.
Lord of life, be in us.
Lord of care, give us awareness.
Let us know and tell and live
        Good News!
Amen, yes, Amen.

GOOD NEWS!

by AL LUSTIE

TARGET

To begin to understand the relationship between what we do and what we are as sharers of Good News.

INTRODUCTION

"DON'T DO AS I DO! DO AS I SAY!" Has an adult ever told you that? Many parents seem to convey this message even if they do not use these words. Unfortunately, as moral instruction it is less than useless. What we are and what we do can influence others a thousand times more than what we say. The only time that what we say is influential is when *what we say* is consistent with *what we are* and *what we do*. Then our words may have tremendous power.

When we think about sharing good news with people, we discover that the best news we bring to most of our acquaintances is ourselves. When people are glad to see us when we walk into the room and they sense something about us that brings love, or respect, or order, or acceptance—that is good news. On the other hand, if our acquaintances cringe when they see us coming, no verbal messages about the love of God will come across as good news from us.

PLANS

BEGINNING WITH GOOD NEWS

After the group has come together, ask each person to introduce himself with his name and some good news he has for this evening. It could go something like: "I'm John Anderson, and my good news tonight is that my dad complimented me earlier today." Persons planning the meeting should be prepared to set an example. It is not necessary to "go around the circle," but as people from here and there share, everyone should have a chance to participate when he or she feels like it.

Then move to a brief discussion of people who share good news. How long has it been since someone in the group heard good news from a friend? Who was the friend? What kinds of good news would this group like to hear? Would it be good news for everybody, or would it be bad news for some? What kind of people seem to be able to share good news in ways that make it come across as GOOD news? What kind of people seem to share good news in ways that make it come across as BAD news?

BREAK INTO SMALL GROUPS

When groups of three or four persons are formed, ask each person to jot down on a piece of paper (not for sharing) a response to this statement: "the kind of good news I'd like in my life someday that I don't have now is. . . ."

Pencil and Paper Needed

After each person has had a chance to think and jot down a response, let the group discuss the phrase "evangelistic life-style." Explain that the word "evangel" has a basic meaning of good news. What would an evangelistic (Good News) life-style be like? What attitudes would a person see in such a life-style? What behaviors? Would a style of life, such as the one we are describing, "ring true" in this group?

After ten or fifteen minutes of discussion, come back into the larger group and report the ways each small group visualizes an evangelistic life-style. Spend a few minutes discussing any differences.

GETTING INVOLVED

Prepare in advance to share the characteristics of the following persons. Duplicates of this page could be made on a copy machine, or the material could be copied on 3″ x 5″ cards.

PETER: A humiliated, forgiven man. Impul-

Prepare in advance

27

sive, given to swearing, not above a little lying, sensitive, weeps when hurt, loves his friends, a bit loud-mouthed.

JIM: Bad-tempered, enjoys being important, comes across a little like an apple-polisher, curses people who don't like him, would like to crowd Peter out at times.

JOHNNIE: Jim's brother, almost as bad-tempered as his brother, is willing to team up with Jim to feel important. Also an apple-polisher, losing his temper easily, but capable of more loving acts than Jim.

Ask for three volunteers who will take the cards and begin acting as if the characteristics on the cards were their personal characteristics. For instance, the Jim cardholder could always try to act like the boss of the group, jump all over people who seem to resent this, etc. These three people will try to behave like Peter, Jim, and Johnnie for the next ten minutes.

Bibles Needed

During this time, encourage the group to read Acts 1:1-8. Point out that in verse 4 there is an order. In verses 5 and 8 there are promises ("you shall receive . . . " "you shall be . . . "). Discuss the relationship of the order ("you must wait . . .") and the three promises. What would all this have to do with an evangelistic life-style? Why should these people wait before rushing out to tell good news? What does the concept "spirit" mean to you? Can you relate it to a football game? A debate? Getting "psyched up" for job-hunting? Is this promise anything you know about personally? What would a person's life-style have to do with his "spirit"?

After ten minutes are over, have the persons behaving like Peter, Jim, and Johnnie end the role playing. Give them their real names back and be sure that they know, and you all know, that they are not in that role any longer. Now discuss for a few minutes: What would it take for these kinds of people (Johnnie, Jim, and Peter)

to be sharers of good news? Realizing that Peter, James, and John were disciples of Jesus (as we are, possibly), what relationship between their needs and Jesus' orders does this group see? In what ways are these relationships valid for us, today?

If there is time, read aloud Acts 2 from a modern translation of the New Testament. Does this sound like a crushed, cranky man? What has happened? Is this the only way to witness to good news?

AN ILLUSTRATION FOR CONCLUSION

"WHAT YOU DO SPEAKS SO LOUDLY THAT I CAN'T HEAR A WORD YOU ARE SAYING." And what you do tells me a lot about who you are. One man stands near the entrance of his church building each Sunday. As people enter to attend church school or the worship service, he confronts them with statements like: "Good morning. Do you know what they're doing now? They're trying to ruin our country. I don't know what the world is coming to! Why, when I was a boy they'd have been horsewhipped!" Total strangers and faithful members run into this tirade every Sunday.

Another man stands near the entrance of his church building. It is a large downtown church with many newcomers attending every Sunday. He has the gift of remembering names, and he greets people as they come in with a pleasant "Good morning" and calls them by name. If they are newcomers, he introduces himself, learns a bit about them, and welcomes them warmly. They will be surprised next week to be greeted by name.

Both men have a life-style. The second man has a good news life-style. The other man needs new power, a new focus, and (dare we say it?) a new spirit before he will ever come across as a bearer of good news.

28

AN EVANGELISTIC LIFE-STYLE
by AL LUSTIE

TARGET

To develop an awareness that an evangelistic life-style can be our life-style.

INTRODUCTION

Charlotte is a woman who spent many months wrestling with her feelings about her son. He was involved in the drug scene. During that time she continued to welcome him home, took homemade bread over to his "pad," and searched for non-coercive ways to love him and his friends. Over the months and years, evangelism was happening. While struggling with her feelings and her half-true ideas, repentance (change of attitude) began happening. At much the same time she recognized the full salvation that was hers in Jesus Christ. As she loved her son and his friends, there were many opportunities to proclaim (quietly) the mighty acts of God. She read of these in her Bible and saw them in the lives of her son's friends. At times she invited one or more of these new acquaintances to decide for Jesus Christ—and some of them did, including her own son. She regularly celebrated the presence of God with other people and was led into deeper and deeper commitments to this Savior-God in the midst of our world. For Charlotte, this effort involved sacrifice. She gave up working full time to work only part time; she has less time for her own projects because it takes time to be a part of God's love; she has let go of some ideas she had held that turned out to be less than true. As Charlotte looks back, she sees an evangelistic life-style emerging in her life that has some of the marks of those Christians mentioned in Acts 8 who never planned to be evangelists. They just lived the way Jesus had taught them to live when hit by their own disaster.

Without waiting for disaster, we are called to live an evangelistic life-style today. The story of Charlotte is true. What will be your story, I wonder?

PLANS

GETTING STARTED

With the whole group together, have someone read Acts 8:1-8 from a modern translation of the New Testament. Plan for a short pause between verses 4 and 5. Then have someone read Acts 11:19-21. Ask the group to respond to these incidents for five minutes or less.

Questions which may help the members focus their responses could include these: Where would you (or your family) go if you were being persecuted in this town for being Christians? Imagine yourselves fleeing to another place; what would you tell people about your reasons for coming? How would you respond to God if one of your family were imprisoned for being a believer and the rest of you were driven out of town? Would you tell your new acquaintances about your "jailbird" relative? What would you tell them?

Now break into small groups of three or four persons each. Make extra copies of this page on a copy machine or have 3" x 5" cards prepared with one of the following definitions on each card: *[handwritten: advance preparation is needed here]*

1. Repentance: establishing a confessional mood which recognizes involvement in the sins of the world.
2. Affirmation: recognizing that there is salvation from these sins in affirming Jesus Christ as Savior and Lord.
3. Proclamation: recognizing that we must declare the mighty acts of God in every setting of life.
4. Invitation: recognizing that this sharing also involves calling others to decide for Jesus, so that they, too, may become what God intends for them as individuals, congregations, or institutions.
5. Celebration: recognizing that a sense of joy and gladness expresses God's transcendent gifts of life now and in the future.
6. Commitment: recognizing the necessity of shifting allegiance from our own self-deter-

mined patterns of living to response to God's patterns of living which we learn through his Son. These patterns include involvement in the needs and oppressions of people in the world.

7. Sacrifice: recognizing the risks involved in living an evangelistic way of life; understanding that God's call is not easy, either personally or corporately. It involves standing with him in the hard places.

Have each group take one topic (or two if the total number of groups is limited). Explain that together these topics make seven characteristics of an evangelistic life-style. Ask each group to read its topic and to work with it awhile. The task is for all persons present to come to personal understandings of what the characteristic they are working with would look like in their lives.

Some questions that could help them might include: If I had this characteristic in my life this coming week, what would it involve? Who would it involve? What would I do differently? What attitudes in me might change? What are the arguments *for* having more of this characteristic in my life, and what are the arguments *against* having more of it in my life?

(It might help to have copies of these questions for each group to use as the members discuss the characteristic[s] they have.)

After about 15 minutes, regroup. Ask each group to share its card along with a few insights the group obtained from the discussion. Put these on newsprint or a chalkboard so that when every group has shared, all seven marks of an evangelistic style of life are before the total group.

OPTIONAL HAPPENING

At this point have two strangers dressed up as policemen or in Gestapo-like uniforms enter the room with clubs and order the group to line up against the wall. Have them read a list of charges against the group that center in its subversive faith and give them twenty-four hours to publicly come out against Christ or leave town. These men then

leave. Give the group about ten minutes to share its feelings about its predicament and ten minutes to discuss plans.

When the time is up, stop the discussion with a repeat reading of Acts 8:1-8. Have the group members reflect on how ready they are to begin living an evangelistic life-style. Then discuss the question: In what ways do we want to begin living an evangelistic life-style this week *without* being forced or persecuted?

Close with a circle in which each person turns to the person on his right and shares an affirmation with him, such as: "Jesus came to give us joy. I'm glad that includes you" or "God loves us all. I'm glad that includes you."

If the optional happening is not possible for your group, do one of the following:

1. Make a large poster-mural with the seven marks of an evangelistic style of life on it. This poster could include illustrations or art work. Plan to display it in your church.
2. Do a group drawing of your church, illustrating what your church would look like if all these marks were evident in your church life. For instance, how would your church people behave if they recognized their involvement in the sins of the world? Can that be drawn?
3. Do a group drawing of your youth group, illustrating what your group would look like if all these marks were evident in your youth group life.
4. Plan a project with a goal of sharing these seven marks of an evangelistic life-style with the whole church. The sharing might be at a morning service, a midweek service, via posters, cassettes, drama, etc. Plan the presentation and if there is time, begin working on it tonight. Carry out your plan.

When you close, form a circle, affirming the person on your right. This could include such phrases as: "Jesus came to bring joy into our lives, (name) _____. I'm glad that includes you. I'm glad it includes me."

WITNESS/INTERPRETER
by EUGENE TON

GOAL

To discover what it means to be a witness/ interpreter of the Christian faith, especially in school.

INTRODUCTION

People seem to have many ideas about what is meant by the word "witnessing." What is witnessing? How does one witness? To what does one witness and why? Is witnessing simply telling someone something? What role does relationship play in witnessing? What is nonverbal witnessing? These and similar questions call attention to our difficulty to respond to the New Testament challenge to be witnesses.

Giving witness is not an option. We are always witnessing. The question is: To what do we witness? Christian witness is developing a style of life which reflects, declares, and experiences God's love. In the words of John's Gospel it is the "Word" becoming flesh. If this is so, then the life of a Christian becomes an interpretation of the gospel message. The way we respond to life situations, the words we speak, the attitudes we carry, the values by which we live all interpret the good news to that portion of the world with which we come in contact. The Christian is an interpretation and an interpreter.

One of the arenas of life open for Christian witness is the school. It is no doubt one of the most difficult, for it is truly the world of "our peers." As a Christian under the imperative to give witness, the challenge is there. But so is guilt, the guilt of failing to meet the challenge. Some of this guilt may come from ignorance.

This program attempts to deal with what witnessing is, particularly in a school setting. Three propositions are advanced for consideration. (Post these propositions in your meeting room.)

- Christian witnessing is an interpretation process. (Note: Interpretation is a two-way process, sending as well as receiving.)
- Christian witnessing involves personal relationships.
- Christian witnessing takes place in the context of life as it is being experienced at that moment.

PLANS

RUMOR GAME

Begin by playing the Rumor Game. The leader shares a rather complicated story of tense human relationships with the person next to him. That opinion is then whispered to the next person and so on until the last person hears it. At that time this person shares aloud what he has heard. Analyze what has happened in the transmission of the opinion and discuss the implications for Christian witnessing. What is implied about the interpretation process? What is needed to interpret adequately a message? Record your observations on newsprint or blackboard.

PROPOSITION STATEMENTS

Share the goal in such a way that each person has an idea of what could occur. Call attention to the proposition statements which have been posted prior to the meeting. Divide into three small groups, assigning one of the proposition statements to each group. The task of each group will be to discuss the statement, what it is saying, whether or not there is agreement and why. Each group can then introduce its statement and give a brief report of the discussion. Again, record observations on the same newsprint or chalkboard.

The following opinion poll should be duplicated or run on a copy machine in advance of the session. Give a copy and a pencil to each person. There are ten statements. Each one should be read and marked in one of the opinion categories.

OPINION POLL					
Statements	I Disagree	I Tend to Disagree	Undecided	I Tend to Agree	I Agree
I think Christian witnessing in school is:					
1. telling someone about the Christian faith.					
2. taking a stand on a school issue, such as busing, drugs, integration, etc.					
3. carrying and reading my Bible.					
4. inviting others to go to my church or youth group.					
5. becoming involved in school life helping to make my school a better school.					
6. affirming the "loners" and those shut out by others.					
7. calling attention to injustices and helping to right them.					
8. becoming a caring person about other persons.					
9. sharing the basis for one's values, principles, and actions in life's situations.					
10. handing out gospel tracts.					

DISCUSS

If your group is large, you may wish to divide into smaller groups to discuss the opinion poll. Taking each statement individually, ask those in the group to share what opinion they marked and why. In the process of discussion relate the opinion discussion to the observations already listed on newsprint or chalkboard.

WORSHIP

Read Acts 8:26-40 from a modern translation.

The passage might be read by asking two persons to take the parts of the Ethiopian and Philip. Another person could read the narrative portions of the selection.

Close with "Passing the Peace." The leader taking the hands of the person nearest to him could share in this manner: "I hope the Christian faith will mean _____ for you." He fills in the statement with what he hopes the faith will mean for the person he is addressing. That person then shares with the one next to him, and so on until the last one has received the peace.

WITNESS/EXCHANGING SELVES

by EUGENE TON

GOAL

To discover some of the dynamics of Christian witnessing and how this relates to witnessing in school.

INTRODUCTION

The charge to witness has long been associated with the Christian movement. New Testament Christians under the power and freshness of the Spirit of God shared their faith eagerly. The church began as a tiny seed and expanded under the impetus of sharing the faith. The missionary zeal and style of the apostle Paul set the stage and pattern by which the Christian church is covering the earth with its witness.

Against this kind of background, we today hear the challenge to witness. Often with guilt nudging us, we ask the question "How?" when the real question may be "What?" What is sharing the faith?

In this meeting we want to discover that witnessing is the exchanging of ourselves with others.

ADVANCE PREPARATION

If you have the S.O.S. Tape #1 *Experimental Study of Selections from the Book of Acts* (Abingdon Press) by Dennis Benson (available at religious bookstores), plan to use the section which gives an interview of a girl living in a commune tell-

ing of her rejection of her former life. Plan to use the blindfold exercise suggested on the tape and have a sufficient number of blindfolds on hand for the group.

PLANS

WRITTEN EXERCISE

After introducing the session and stating the goal, ask each person to make a list of all the ways that come to mind by which he or she is influenced by others. Opposite each form of influence he should indicate whether that influence is helpful or not helpful.

DISCUSSION

Ask each one to share his or her list with the leader and record the lists on newsprint or chalkboard. Be sure to ask whether each way of influence was helpful or unhelpful and why. Lead your group in a discussion of the relationship between the ways we are influenced and Christian witnessing, particularly in school. Some questions which may be used are: "How is one influenced?" "What takes place in the influencing process?" "What insight does this give us into Christian witnessing?" Record these insights on a separate newsprint headed: Insights into Christian Witnessing.

BLINDFOLD EXERCISE

At this time blindfold each person present indicating that you will be engaging in another exercise which may help in understanding what is involved in Christian witnessing. When all the blindfolds are in place, read Acts 9:10-19 (NEB). In silence allow each person to think about what has been read, trying to identify the feelings of blindness and someone coming to help. Talk about these feelings.

If you have the tape listed under "Advance Preparation," listen to the girl from a commune explain how she is trying to save her sanity. With the blindfolds still in place, lead your group in a discussion of the question: If this girl were a close friend of mine, what could I do for her? If you do not have this tape, use another illustration of a person searching for new values.

After all have had the opportunity to share their response, have a preselected girl go to each blindfolded person, take his or her hands in hers, and say with great emotion, "Help me!" Again have your group members discuss what they think could be done for the girl. It is hoped the responses in this discussion will be more personal and authentic because there has been an interchange of persons.

Blindfolds can now be removed. Discuss what insights have been gained about Christian witnessing through this experience. List these expressions under the heading "Insights into Christian Witnessing" on the newsprint where you have listed the forms of influence.

WORSHIP

The leader should sum up the insights. Read Acts 9:17 and 18. Like Paul you have been given sight. In a spirit of worship ask each person to write down what he or she has to give the school world tomorrow. In prayer and commitment these papers can be received as an offering to God.

THE MEANING OF PENTECOST
by ROBERT P. MEYE

TARGET

To understand better the meaning of the church's experience of Pentecost, especially as it is described for us in Acts 2.

PENTECOST

If, as is often said, there is great ignorance among Christians regarding the person and significance of the Holy Spirit (otherwise described as Holy Ghost, Spirit of God, or simply The Spirit), there is even greater ignorance regarding the meaning of Pentecost.

We need first of all to be aware of the meanings of the word "Pentecost" itself:

1. "Pentecost" is a word used to describe one of the three great "feasts" of the church calendar. It is celebrated seven weeks after Easter.
2. The word "Pentecost" literally means "fiftieth" in the Greek. Among early Christians (and others) who spoke Greek, it was used to describe the fiftieth day after the Passover (the time of Jesus' death).
3. For our purposes in this session, we need to take note of the adjective "pentecostal." Many Christians speak of a "pentecostal experience"; for many this term is used to describe a unique experience which is *like that* described in Acts 2.

If there are many Christians who have only a vague idea as to how to think of the Holy Spirit, there are also many scholars who are equally perplexed when they seek to understand what happened in Jerusalem to the disciples of Jesus after Easter on that first great day of Pentecost. We must be satisfied to seek only *some* ideas about Pentecost and its meaning.

PLANS

BIBLE STUDY

1. Have each person in the group imagine himself or herself to be one of Jesus' disciples after Easter. This was the greatest day in history for those disciples. Their wonderful friend had been killed and buried—and God raised him. He was not simply "back from the dead"—he was *the Living One!* He forgave them—they had betrayed him. He walked and talked and ate with them and spoke of the great future— the same Jesus with whom some of them had lived several years.

Imagine yourselves to be the disciples planning for the future. What would *you* do? What *could* you do?

2. Now, turn to Luke 24:44-49 and Acts 1:1-8 and read these passages aloud. Observe that Jesus instructed the disciples not to do anything until the Spirit should come. What do these texts teach about the Holy Spirit? Why do you feel that *power* is the key word describing the meaning of the Spirit for those earliest Christians (as in Acts 1:8)? Relate the meaning of power in Acts 1:8 to the many ways in which "power" is used today (student power, black power, people power). How do these kinds of power differ from mechanical power?

3. Now read Acts 2:1-16. What events or *phenomena* marked the coming of the Holy Spirit?

4. For discussion:
   - What do you think the disciples expected to happen?
   - How do you connect "speaking in tongues" (Acts 2:4, 6, 11) to the promise of Acts 1:8? What was "powerful" about *this* experience?
   - What was the immediate result of speaking in tongues? (Read Acts 2:41-47.)

A NOTE ON "TONGUES" (GLOSSOLALIA)

"Speaking in tongues" (glossolalia) is not unique to the book of Acts. Throughout the history of the church there have been instances of this phenomenon. Moreover, non-Christian religions and cultural groups also have had this experience.

There is apparently no one answer to the question "What is speaking in tongues?" To critics, tongues are "gibberish" or "ecstatic ejaculation" or "nonsense syllables." To those who experience them, tongues are a "second blessing" or a "powerful experience of God." Linguists have not found any resemblance to actual known languages. Suffice it to say that these strange speech sounds are for some Christians an expression of the (always powerful) presence and work of the Spirit emerging in a person's life.

A CONTEMPORARY PROBLEM

There are many Christians today who give testimony to the common experiences of "speaking in tongues." Often those who have this experience testify that it is one of the most wonderful things that ever happened to them and urge others to seek this same experience of the Holy Spirit. Other

Christians believe that speaking in tongues is not so important or that it belonged to the first century only, and they fear lest the chief effect of speaking in tongues today be the creation of division within the churches. How are we to live with the text of Acts and with the increasing debate in our own time?

Always remember the following observations, and they will help you answer the questions above:

1. Remember that Jesus himself was a man of the Spirit (read Mark 1:6-11), but the Gospels do not describe him as one who spoke in tongues.
2. Remember that God has special gifts for special times (read Acts 2:16-18).
3. Remember that the apostle Paul said that love should be our highest aim (read 1 Corinthians 14:1) and that speaking so as to be understood is more important than speaking in tongues (read 1 Corinthians 14:19).
4. Remember that the early Christians *did* receive the gift of speaking in tongues as the Holy Spirit was present in their lives (read from Acts 2; 1 Corinthians 12:10).
5. Remember that every gift of the Spirit has value only if it is accepted and used to build up the body of Christ (read Acts 2:41-42—the result

of the apostle's earlier speaking in tongues— and also 1 Corinthians 14:12).

SOLUTION

Remember all this from the Bible and be free to ask for God the Holy Spirit to work in you as he wills—and no one should criticize what you receive from the hand of God! The Bible teaches two things clearly—that the Holy Spirit works as he wills (John 3:8) and that we should not resist the Spirit (1 Thessalonians 5:19).

A PROJECT

Do you have any acquaintances who belong to a "pentecostal" church or group? You might ask them to share their understanding of Acts 2 and its meaning for them. Some people in all churches, including Roman Catholics, are involved in "speaking in tongues" nowadays.

DISCUSSION

In view of the five reminders above, can one be content to live as a Christian without speaking in tongues? How important is the pattern of Jesus' life for you?

THE HOLY SPIRIT

by ROBERT P. MEYE

TARGET

To understand better the meaning of Christian belief in the Holy Spirit.

INTRODUCTION

You have perhaps heard of the man who, when asked to describe God, said, "I knew very well who he was until you asked me." Unfortunately, many who confess belief in God carry around a very hazy conception of the Holy Spirit. (Right here we should note that there are also other ways of speaking of the Holy Spirit, such as, "Spirit of God," "the Spirit," "the Holy Ghost," "God's Spirit," "the Spirit of Christ.")

PLANS

Pencils and paper will be needed as the group responds to the following task.

Can you list five words which come to your mind when you think of the Holy Spirit—or which help you to describe to others how you understand the Holy Spirit? Don't be embarrassed about your words, no matter how strange or unlearned the list may seem. If you read in church history or even in the Bible, you will find that men who have been moved and blessed by the Spirit of God have often been ridiculed and misunderstood by others. The Old Testament prophets are a classic example of this fact; so was Jesus. And sometimes even Christians find it difficult to accept ways which other Christians attribute to the Holy Spirit.

THE HOLY SPIRIT AND THE APOSTLES' CREED

Even though they may not have a clear idea of the Holy Spirit, many Christians throughout the world regularly confess their belief in the Holy Spirit as they recite the Apostles' Creed together at worship each Sunday. Do you know the Apostles' Creed? Here is the so-called "Third Article" of the Creed which focuses on the Holy Spirit:

I believe in the Holy Spirit,

The holy Catholic Church
  [*reference is to church universal, not Roman Catholic*],
The communion of saints,
The forgiveness of sins,
The resurrection of the body,
And the life everlasting.   Amen.

All these items are to be understood in special relation to the first line, which speaks of the Holy Spirit.

Now in a group of friends compare your answers to the question about your understanding of the Holy Spirit with the items in this creedal statement. Did you have even one of the items mentioned in the creed on your own list of words to be associated with the Holy Spirit? How were your lists different than the creedal list? Can you guess why this is so? (For example, is the creedal material more biblical in its orientation? Is it more concrete?)

The important lesson to be learned here is that we should not think about the Holy Spirit apart from those things which are important in our everyday life as Christians. Some of these, as suggested in the creed, are: the church of which we become a part when we believe in Christ; forgiveness of sins for which we pray daily; the fellowship of God's people which supports and nourishes us in the world; the resurrection and eternal life—the great experiences through which the Christian will enter some day into a whole new order of existence.

WHO IS THE HOLY SPIRIT?

The program leader may wish to use the following as an introduction to Bible study.

Jesus once told one of his disciples that seeing him was the same as seeing the Father. The same could be said of the relationship between Jesus and the Holy Spirit. The Holy Spirit is nothing less than God with us, Christ with us. Any understanding of the Holy Spirit that misses this point is not biblically informed.

The earliest Christians had many of the same experiences that we do, and they reported them to be a result of the Holy Spirit working in their lives. Their belief in the Holy Spirit was the means by which they understood the great and good things which were happening to them (as well as those things which they did).

- Do we have experiences in our lives that we can understand only as experiences of the presence of God? Read 2 Corinthians 1:21, 22, and Acts 2:38.

- Do we believe that God has worked in our lives for good? Read Galatians 5:15-25, especially verse 22.

- Do we believe that God has somehow bound us in a special way to other persons who have also trusted Christ? Read 1 Corinthians 12:13 and Romans 8:14-17.

In reading these texts and many others like them you can see how early Christians did not claim their common experiences for themselves but gratefully saw the work of the Spirit of God everywhere in their lives. That made them different!

THE HOLY SPIRIT TODAY

Pair off and share your faith with a friend in the following way.

Share what you think is the greatest thing that God has ever done in your life.

Then share one small quality change in your life which you have reason to believe is the result of someone else's help.

Once you have done this, regather as a larger group. Let each person share with the group that which is appropriate from what his companion shared with him or her. Share what you feel will be helpful to the total group and try not to embarrass your partner.

Now, recognize the fact that if you were a Christian in the first century, you would understand that these things were the result of the Holy Spirit working in your lives.

FURTHER REFLECTION ON THE WORK OF THE HOLY SPIRIT

As you have time, read and discuss either 1 Corinthians 12:7-11 (regarding the gifts of the Spirit) or Galatians 5:22-24 (regarding the fruit of the Spirit). You might even study both passages and ask how they relate to one another.

The leader now calls attention to sheets of newsprint scattered around the room. The following concerns should be written, one on each of the four pieces of newsprint: "Gifts of the Spirit we need are. . . ." "Fruits of the Spirit we need are . . . because. . . ." "I feel God's Spirit calls us to. . . ." "The mission of our youth fellowship, our church, should be to. . . ." A magic marker should be provided at each newsprint location.

Divide the total group into four groups. (If this makes the subgroups too small, adjust the plan.) Have groups move to each of the newsprint locations and react to the statement in writing. After five minutes have them choose one person to stay with the newsprint and the rest move on (counterclockwise) to the next location. The concern and the first group's response is then interpreted by the person who stayed at the newsprint. The new group responds to this and adds its own insights to the newsprint. At a signal from the leader a different person is chosen to remain behind. Another move is made, and the task is repeated. If time allows, this could be done one more time. When the program is over, an opportunity should be provided for all to look at all newsprints to see what happened after they left them.

CLOSING PRAYER

"Come, Holy Spirit, Come. Come, Lord, like a fire and burn; come, Lord, like the wind and cleanse. Convert, convince, consecrate us till we are wholly Thine. Amen."

40

WHY IS DISCIPLINE NECESSARY IN THE CHRISTIAN FAITH?

by DAVID E. CLOUD

PURPOSE

To see the significance of spiritual disciplines in the life of a maturing Christian. (Post on chalkboard or newsprint.)

GETTING THE PICTURE

Recruit three volunteer youth to stand in an informal cluster at the front of the room on the left side, and two adults to stand on the right side of the room.

TEEN 1: Discipline? Ugh! I hate it.

TEEN 2: Makes me think of my parents.

TEEN 3: Sounds like teachers. You can have them.

ADULT 1: Some young people experience discipline as punishment.

ADULT 2: True. And others see it as being required over and over again to do something they don't wish to do.

ADULT 1: I don't blame them for hating discipline.

ADULT 2: The problem is that negative experiences gang up on them and cut them off from potentially good and wholesome experiences with discipline.

ADULT 1: Well, at least they can see their inner doors beginning to open when they picture themselves as Christian.

TEEN 1: What does "inner door" mean? I don't get it!

ADULT 1: For me it is the door to personhood, the door to the center of self.

ADULT 2: I guess then they see the need for accepting one or more specific faith disciplines into their daily lives.

TEEN 2: What do you mean by "faith discipline"?

ADULT 2: Some examples of faith discipline would be prayer, Bible study, Christian social action, and practicing love.

ADULT 3: If the image of the Christian they want to be is being patterned after some Christian hero, such as a biblical or contemporary personality, their inner doors swing open more widely, and discipline is openly desired and joyfully practiced.

TEEN 3: Are you sure about that?

ADULT 1: I can see that cultivating the desire for a high self-image is a necessary, ongoing task if Christian disciplines are to be effective.

ALL THREE TEENS: Discipline? BAH!

PLANS

MATCHING GAME

Advance Preparation Needed

Divide the group into smaller search groups of four or five persons. Give each group a large (2 x 3 foot) newsprint and a felt marker. Divide each sheet with a line down the center. On the left side write the heading "I Can Teach," and on the right side write "I Want to Learn."

Allow up to ten minutes for everyone in each group to list one or two items in each column. Then ask one or more of the groups to make a list of what has made it possible for them to say they can teach someone something. The remaining groups are to discuss why they cannot do what they have said they want to learn.

After five minutes, call for each group's report. Keep a record of the number of times some aspect of discipline is mentioned and share the summary with the group. Look for an implied use of discipline.

STORY

Explain that the following story about the presence or lack of discipline in Doug's life has no conclusion. Writing a conclusion is the task of the group.

Doug was an excellent athlete in three sports,

having lettered two years in each so far. He wants to become a professional football player after college competition. During his senior year in high school he started running around with a fast crowd which enjoyed late night joy rides and drinking beer. He was arrested for driving under the influence, got his name in the newspaper, and had his driver's license suspended. His father is trying to use his influence to get the suspension revoked.

Have small subgroups prepare to act out a one-minute conclusion to the story, using one of the three questions as a guide.

The following persons might be portrayed: Doug, the coach, teammates, a Christian friend, Doug's father and mother.

- What do you think the coach said when he found out?
- What did the team do?
- How might a Christian boy relate to Doug's special need?

Applaud each one-minute "production" at its conclusion in support of those who risked coming before the total group.

DISCUSSION

How realistic were the roles being played? Were the solutions practical, helpful, unreal, or destructive? How did you feel playing the role assigned? What has this role play taught us about Christian disciplines? How might one or more of the Christian disciplines (prayer, worship, Bible study, giving of self in love to others) have helped Doug? Be specific.

QUESTIONNAIRE

Why discipline? (Place the following questionnaire on newsprint or use an overhead projector, or use it as a litany in this session and for reference in the following sessions on discipline.)

Ask for a show of hands on each of the ten items by saying, "How many believe that number _____ is a valid reason for having discipline in the Christian faith?" Write the number with a felt marker on the line provided. After individuals have responded to the ten questions, their scores will be recorded.

1. _____ To develop trust in others.
2. _____ To gain self-control.
3. _____ To accomplish personal goals.
4. _____ To have happiness.
5. _____ To find life's lasting values.
6. _____ To be a responsible citizen.
7. _____ To be ready in a crisis.
8. _____ To reach maturity.
9. _____ To become fully human with others.
10. _____ To know and obey God's will.

Advance Preparation Needed Here

Encourage discussion about any differences in the number of votes for the various items. Allow freedom for variances of opinion.

WORSHIP

Read Matthew 6:25-33.

Use the list above as a closing prayer (litany). The whole group begins with "Lord, help me to develop trust in others." Then use "Thank you, God" as a response after each phrase.

ASSIGNMENT (a challenge to use discipline)

Everyone select one area of life where faith discipline is needed and practice that discipline for a whole week. See what God does with you. Give him thanks.

WHAT FAITH DISCIPLINES
SHOULD THE CHRISTIAN PRACTICE?
by DAVID E. CLOUD

PURPOSE

To explore what it means to be a Christian and which faith disciplines are needed to be effective. (Post this on newsprint or chalkboard.)

GETTING THE PICTURE

Ask: What does it mean to be an apprentice worker on a job? (A person who learns the skills of a trade while helping with or while doing the work.) Those who accept Jesus Christ as their Savior at a young age have a lifelong vocation of becoming like him, the master teacher. To be an apprentice to Jesus is not easy.

Write the following emphasized words on the chalkboard as you use them in giving this background material: Jesus *demonstrated* the values of such an *in-service training program* for us today. Recall his selection of twelve men and the informal and formal training he arranged for them. For example, they asked, "Master, teach us to *pray*." And he did. Jesus' own *worship* habits, patterns of *Scripture study,* and the *giving* of *himself* to meet the *needs* of others built a solid foundation for ac-

cepting, believing, and obeying his verbal teaching.

They saw and later experienced the reserves of *power, wisdom,* and *courage* which came from keeping in constant touch with the Father, God. Jesus said that his followers would do even greater things than he. That group includes young people and adults today.

PLUNGING INTO THE SESSION *Advance Preparation Needed Here*
COLLAGE

Here is one way to get at what the group understands a Christian to be and what he does. Have a sheet of newsprint for each grouping of four or five persons. Also provide a supply of magazines, scissors, glue, crayons, and watercolor paints. Ask the members to use any one or all of the materials on the table to describe on the newsprint sheet what they see as the ideal Christian—what he is like as a person, what he does.

After fifteen or twenty minutes have the groups share their "portrait of a Christian." What do the collages say Christians do? Are faith disciplines noted? Why or why not?

ACROSTIC

(This is a way to determine the group's familiarity with faith disciplines and their application.)

Write the letters D-I-S-C-I-P-L-I-N-E-S under each other along the left side of the chalkboard. Ask members to suggest rapidly words which they feel are related to the various faith disciplines, one or more for each letter. The resulting acrostic may be used in a closing worship service.

Here is a sample acrostic, with added explanation:

D *oubting doubts* (challenge them in order to strengthen one's faith in God)

I *nspiration* through *worship* services (gives one the motivation to serve God with joy)

S *cripture reading and study* (being open to God's truth)

C *onfession of sin* (humility before God, readiness to serve)

I *nspiration*—private *meditation* (thinking God-thoughts)

P *rayer* for self and others (keeping the power line open)

L *iving for others* (responsible action, including suffering)

I *nspiration* (seeing God's truth wherever it may be found)

N *eed to witness* (at all times and places, by life and word)

E *nabling* personal *resources* to be used for God's purposes, in church and the community (time, talent, treasure)

S *tudy* and *search* and *question* in the quest for harmony in God's plan (resources other than the Bible)

DISCUSSION

Which faith disciplines do the words refer to? Which are the most useful, practical? Which are easy and which are hard? What are the benefits?

USE OF DISCIPLINE

Have the group look over the acrostic for ways to get soul food and count the number of faith disciplines with which they have had experience. Ask them to hold up the number of fingers which corresponds to the number they have experienced. Record the numbers on the target as in the diagram. If two have experienced one or two, write 2 on the first band around the target.

Then ask, "How many of them do you want to experience?" Again, take a count and record on the target.

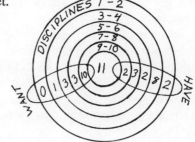

Discuss what is the relationship between the HAVES and the WANTS. Are they alike or are they widely different on any band? If there are quite a number who want more experience, ask them to share what they feel is keeping them from the experience now. Offer any help you can.

WORSHIP

Ask one or more students to read the specified Bible passages at the appropriate time during the devotional talk. Have them stand or sit at different places around the room.

Share: To be a Christian is to live a certain way of life—the life which is pleasing to God (John 8:28-29). The foundation for that life is a person (Jesus, Luke 6:47-49). Christians cannot grow unless they eat of God's Word daily. How strong, healthy, and energetic would we be if we only ate one meal a week on Sundays?

So it is with that part of us which is created in God's image, our spiritual natures. "Slavery to God," said St. Augustine, "is perfect freedom" (John 8:31-32, 36). Bible study, prayer, worship, meditation, and giving of our resources to meet the needs of persons are some of the ways we are given the perfect freedom to become the mature selves God created us to be.

Accepting faith disciplines may cause the Christian to experience some unpleasantness (Romans 8:17). Dave Wilkerson of Teen Challenge says, "Enough of this frivolous joy-pop feeling for Jesus.

. . . Jesus has to be a way of dying before He can become a way of living."[1]

Close in a friendship circle with a period of silent meditation, interrupted every fifteen or twenty seconds with a short question for thought: "How satisfied am I with my Christian faith? After this time together, will my life be any different? Am I willing to go further on the journey into my soul? If not, what will I do?" Close with a short prayer and everyone singing "Amazing Grace."

EVALUATION

After the meeting, but before anyone leaves, post or call attention to the following questions, which have been prepared ahead of time. Encourage everyone to respond. Explain that you will use the information to plan further meetings on this subject and that you will be available to anyone who wishes to discuss what he or she wrote.

1. Write one spiritual success you have had in your lifetime.
2. Write one of your spiritual disappointments.
3. Has this meeting helped clarify any questions you have had about faith disciplines? How? (Be specific.)
4. What would you like more help with in your spiritual life?
5. From whom would you like to receive help?

[1] David Wilkerson, *The Jesus Restoration* (Old Tappan, New Jersey: Fleming H. Revell Company, 1972), p. 8.

SHOULD FAITH DISCIPLINE BE EXTERNAL OR INTERNAL?

by DAVID E. CLOUD

PURPOSE

To clarify the source of one's faith discipline. (Post this on newsprint or chalkboard.)

PHYSICAL WARM-UP

Have outdoor or indoor games, or do some stretches, bends, and jumps together as a group. Laugh and enjoy the loosening up.

GETTING THE PICTURE

IMAGINATION GAME

(The leader should practice the game before trying to lead it in order to get the feel of how to time the suggestions and questions.)

In a low-pitched, calm, and very relaxed voice give these instructions: Have everyone either sit or lie on the floor in a very relaxed position, away from each other. Darken the room somewhat so the bright lights do not distract. Have all persons close their eyes. Suggest that they listen and feel their own breathing—allow one minute. Ask them to imagine that they are rocks. Every fifteen or twenty seconds ask a question to encourage them to clarify their mental picture: What is it like to be a rock? How heavy a rock are you? What color are you? What can you do as a rock? What would you like to do? What does it feel like to be a rock?

Suggest that they begin to come back to reality, still with their eyes closed. Allow silence between the instructions: Listen again to your own breathing. Can you feel the breath moving in your lungs? You may want to reach out to touch the floor (or the seat you are sitting in). After thirty seconds, turn on the lights gradually, maybe a light from another room first.

DISCUSSION

Ask: How did you feel? Allow all those who volunteer to share their feelings. What decisions did you make in your imaginary experience? What caused you to make them (an outside force, or from within)? List the suggested causes on the chalkboard or newsprint under these headings:

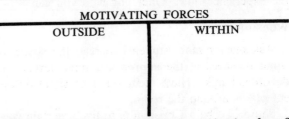

MOTIVATING FORCES	
OUTSIDE	WITHIN

How did you feel about each motivating force? Place a "G" beside those they feel *good* about, and an "S" beside those which are rated *so-so,* and an "R" beside those rated *rotten.*

What do their feelings say about whom they want to make decisions in their lives? Others or self, mostly? A balance? Suggestions from others and the final decision by the self?

ROLE PLAY

Ask for three or four persons to volunteer to be in a role-play situation dealing with making a decision about the use or nonuse of a faith discipline—offering to lead the mealtime prayer at home.

Characters needed:

MR. CROWN (father)—He runs the home with a stern hand, does not appear to have deep religious beliefs, though he attends worship fairly regularly and the Men's Bible Class to be with his friends.

MRS. CROWN (mother)—A warm, open person, appears religious.

DEE (daughter)—Junior high age, attends church, withholds her feelings and beliefs.

PAUL (son)—Senior high, very active at church, has learned to pray there.

SETTING—Sunday noon dinner. The whole family went to church earlier. Mr. Crown asks one of the children to give the mealtime prayer. What happens next?

DISCUSSION

What decisions were made? (List them on the chalkboard by the name of the family member who made them.) How did each decision affect the others around the table? How did the players feel toward the other play members? Which decisions helped? Which ones hurt?

Ask the observing members to give the players various suggestions as to new behavior which they feel would improve relationships in the Crown home. List these on the newsprint. Ask the players how they feel about the suggestions. *Role-play* the same situation with the players adopting any new behavior which they feel will contribute to better family relations.

Then discuss what helped the family. What slowed down or stopped progress in decision-making? Place the group's ideas on the chalkboard:

Helped	Slowed Down/Stopped

Ask the players who tried out new behavior to share how they feel about it.

APPLICATION

What do the findings on decision-making which were discovered during this session tell us about where our discipline in the Christian faith should come from? External or internal, or both? Look around the room at our newsprint lists and thoughtfully consider your answer.

Whatever your decision, you have to live with it, but not alone. How can we be supportive of one another at school, home, work, church, play, in our decision-making as maturing Christians?

MEDITATION AND FOLLOW THROUGH

Read 1 John 2:3-6. Ask yourself: If I took this Scripture passage seriously, what would I do this week that I haven't done before in the area of faith discipline? Put your name on your paper. Write down your thoughts. Be specific. We'll mail the paper back to you in a week so you can check out your behavior. You may want to continue making some alterations in the weeks ahead. (Collect the sheets.)

Everyone stand, cross arms, and join hands in a friendship circle. Place the papers in the center of the circle on the floor. Focus attention on the papers while singing the song "You've Got a Friend." Each time the word "friend" is sung, let your eyes move to join the eyes of a friend in the circle. Flash a short, unspoken prayer for him or her, especially in regard to the special need expressed on the sheet of paper which is lying on the floor.

CHRISTIAN BELIEF AND THE OCCULT

by ROGER C. PALMS

TARGET

To understand why the occult is so attractive to people and to help Christians think through what they know about it.

INTRODUCTION

Have you ever knocked on wood? Have you had a hunch that turned out to be true? Have you seen amazing truth in your horoscope? Every time you cross your fingers, say a prayer, or read your "stars" in the paper, you express your belief in some kind of supernatural power. The crux of the issue is whether or not the supernatural power of God can be separated from the powers of the occult.

If you ask some occult believers why they have gone into the occult as a religious belief, their answers will sound almost Christian.

"It is a way to experience miracles!"

"Prayer is important to me, and prayer is really mental telepathy."

"When I contact the spirit world, I'm doing what Jesus did when he talked with Moses and Elijah on the Mount of Transfiguration."

"Witches' covens are a warm fellowship."

"Ouija boards are a type of divine revelation."

People are flocking to the many types of occult religious practices because they say that these help them to find God. And some of these people claim to be Christians.

But people who have left the occult to become Christians teach that the occult is Satan's way of drawing people to himself while letting them think that they are discovering God. People in the occult are always seeking God, but seldom turn to him by way of Jesus Christ.

This program will deal with the Christian's reaction to the occult and help him discover Christian resources for teaching others about the occult.

PLANS

GETTING INVOLVED

"What's wrong with having a seance?" a Christian mother asked her son and daughter who seemed so alarmed over the proposed plans for their younger sister's overnight camping trip.

"Saturday night they are going to have a seance at the campfire. It's just for fun; they'll enjoy themselves."

FACING THE ISSUE

As the group sits on the floor or in chairs in a circle, talk about the younger sister's planned seance with her friends. What is your first reaction? As the group begins to wrestle with this story (and it's a true story), the different information and feelings that each person has about the occult will become apparent. Don't argue with each other, but listen to what each person says.

DISCUSSION

What would you do if this were your sister? Would you care that she is going to get involved in a seance? What would you say to her? What would you say to your mother about the seance?

MIND BENDERS

Passing out Bibles, let each person look up one or more of the references listed. These references should be made available in advance. The Scriptures tell of Satan's power, demonism, and who Jesus is.

Leviticus 19:31
Deuteronomy 18:10-13
Matthew 13:19
Acts 8:18-24
Ephesians 6:10-13
Philippians 2:6-11
Colossians 1:11-20
James 4:7-8
1 Peter 5:8-10
1 John 3:8
1 John 5:18-19
Revelation 12:9

Advance Preparation Needed

Bibles Needed

When each person is equipped with a passage of Scripture, all may serve as prompters while two people dialogue the following three encounter experiences with the younger sister.

1. The sister comes home from the camping trip and announces that the seance was a success. They had indeed contacted the spirit world, and she is happy about some wonderful directions given to her by departed spirits. They told her how she could better prepare for her future.

Her brother (or sister) must respond to her. What should that response be? The brother (or sister) can dialogue with the "younger sister" as long as he or she feels qualified and then yield to someone else in the group who can dialogue, using Scripture as a reference point. This person responds until someone else takes his or her place.

Whoever plays the role of the little sister should not be silly or an arguer. Let her simply be convinced of her position.

2. The younger sister comes home and announces that the seance was a failure. She says that there is nothing to this occult business and that anyone who says that he can contact the spirit world must be stupid. She denies that there is any reality to occult belief.

Again, one at a time, people play the role of the older brother or sister, each one speaking as he or she feels qualified.

3. The sister comes home and announces that although the seance didn't work, she is certain that contacting the departed spirits in the spirit world is like prayer, only greater. Instead of just talking to God, she believes that she can talk to many people in heaven to get their views on things. She intends to try it often to "improve my Christian life."

Each of these three encounter situations will require listening, understanding, and responding lovingly (not arguing, ridiculing, or criticizing). The experience will show how attractive the occult can be, how difficult it is to pinpoint the problems in it, and will create an awareness of the spectrum of Scripture that relates directly or indirectly to the occult.

DISCOVERY

Dividing into buzz groups, let each group discuss one of the following questions:
1. Where do you think casual dabbling in the occult leads?

2. How does the word "supernatural" make you feel? What first comes to mind? Do you react positively or negatively?
3. Is there a force in today's world we can call Satan?
4. Do you believe Satan manipulates people by means of a seance?
5. If persons contact the spirit world once, do you feel they will want to do it again?
6. Do you think a person who tries a seance also would want to try other forms of occult religion, like visiting mediums, following astrology charts, practicing spells in witchcraft, or even making a pact with Satan if it will give him "power" or "guidance"?
7. Do you believe a person could discover Jesus through the occult?

Ask each group to bring back its answers to the larger group, sharing the consensus of opinions given in the buzz group.

WRAP-UP

Supplies Needed

Unrolling a long piece of shelf paper on a table or the floor and passing out pencils or crayons, let each person take one section of the paper for his work space (single sheets will do, but there is value in working closely together). On his section of the paper, each person should list every reason he or she can think of why Christians might be tempted to try one of the occult practices.

When everyone is finished, each person can read his reasons out loud to the whole group. When all of the reasons have been shared, one person can ask the whole group: "Does anyone have a reason on his paper that Jesus Christ cannot satisfy or answer if people would trust him instead?" Several people may think that they do have a reason that Jesus cannot satisfy or answer; if so let the group members discuss it and draw their own conclusions.

WORSHIP

Forming a circle, pray for each other. Mention the person on your right by name asking that he will stay close to Jesus Christ for the guidance and direction he needs in his life.

THERE IS NO HERE AND THERE

by RUSSELL E. BROWN

TARGET

To understand that the nature of the gospel involves us in the whole world and that today there are many avenues for youth in world involvement.

INTRODUCTION

"God so loved *the world*. . . ." There cannot be peace in the U.S.A. while war is raging in Asia. Or in Nigeria. Or on the Gaza Strip. Any Good News from God in this country has to be Good News for all mankind. If it is for one continent or one race or one nation only, it is not from God. As we intensify our proclamation of Christ as Lord in our own communities, will we also honor and proclaim him as Lord of the whole world?

PLANS

PLAN FOR THE UNIT

This session is the first of three programs dealing with the present situation in the world mission of the Christian church. The first session deals with personal involvement. The second session will consider how we can be supportive of others, both American missionaries and national church leaders of other nations, in the work they are doing. The third session will discuss how the gospel relates to the developing nations and the meeting of the physical needs of people.

If you want to use these programs as a unit, you will want to plan ahead. A film or filmstrip would be helpful for either the second or third session in this series. The following are possible sources for audio-visuals:

1. Consult your denomination's listing of films and filmstrips on missions.
2. Persuade your church to purchase the filmstrip entitled *Crusade Against Hunger,* from Agricultural Missions, Inc., 475 Riverside Drive, New York, NY 10027. $5.00.
3. Write to Japan International Christian University Foundation for materials on the work of

that institution (475 Riverside Drive, New York, NY 10027).
4. Filmstrips on missions may be available in your community, from church audio-visual libraries, or ecumenical agencies.

PREPARING FOR THIS MEETING

1. Have any adults in your church worked overseas for a private firm? If so, perhaps you could invite them to tell of any opportunities they found for Christian fellowship and service overseas.
2. If you have men in your church who in military service overseas found opportunity for Christian fellowship or worship, ask them to tell about it.
3. Look for reports from students who have been in a Junior Year Abroad program or who have traveled abroad. Invite foreign students to speak to your group.
4. Do some research about influences—religious and otherwise—that the United States is currently experiencing from Asia, Africa, or Latin America. For example: The Bahai Movement, Yoga or various forms of Hindu meditation, the Krishna Consciousness Cult, Zen Buddhism, Soka Gakkai.
5. Ask your pastor about the "Laymen Abroad" program, or Union Churches Overseas, or write for information about this to Committee on Laymen Abroad, Division of Overseas Ministries, 475 Riverside Drive, New York, NY 10027.
6. Check your denominational publications for articles on missions.

MEETING OUTLINE

THOUGHT STIMULATORS

Have a display table with materials or pictures on any of the above movements from overseas that are influencing the U.S.A., or on your church's mission program overseas, on students abroad, or laymen abroad programs. Ask the young people as individuals or in small groups to look over materials for about ten minutes and report back.

BRAINSTORMING

1. You have probably heard people say:

"We have enough problems here at home without getting involved with the rest of the world."

"We need to clean up our own backyard before we can set out to save the rest of the world."

The fact is that there is no "here" nor "there" in this world. We are constantly affecting each other around the world. For example:

When there was a dock strike in New York City, within a day or two the Volkswagen factory in Germany had to shut down.

To stop traffic in heroin in the U.S.A., agents must stop the sources in Southeast Asia.

Because of the need for doctors and nurses in the U.S.A. there is a large immigration of doctors from India and nurses from the Philippines each year.

2. Describe some of the following and tell why they have become popular today in the U.S.A.: Karate, Yoga, the signs of the Zodiac, the Bahai faith, Krishna Consciousness. Are these indications of the impact of Asian ideas on the U.S.A.?

3. With airplanes traveling all over the world, what means are used to prevent epidemics of disease from spreading through air travel?

4. Some people say: "Trying to spread Christianity is interfering in other people's lives."

With world trade, international business, and travel on the increase, should Christianity be quarantined in the U.S.A.? Does the American leave his Christianity at home on the shelf when he goes overseas? Or is carrying the gospel everyone's task?

REPORTS

Laymen Abroad Program. This program seeks to provide orientation for Christians who will be living overseas, to help them understand the culture and relate to the people with a positive Christian witness.

English-speaking churches overseas. Many large cities of the world have an American union church or an English language church which provides fellowship and ministry to Americans working in that culture.

Junior Year Abroad programs of American colleges.

Work camps or other special work and service opportunities for youth overseas.

EXAMPLE: A Presbyterian layman, an engineer, had the opportunity to put in a bid for his firm for a sewage system for the city of Bangkok, Thailand. His firm got the job, and he was able to save the city several million dollars over what other firms would have charged. When the job was done, the mayor of Bangkok, a Buddhist, called in the American engineer and asked him why he was willing to help save the city several million dollars in their installation costs. Can you imagine what this Christian engineer replied? After he had given his witness to honesty in business, the mayor replied, "Then let us give thanks to the Christian God for your coming to help us."[1]

EXAMPLE: Recently Miss Bethene Trexel, a college girl from Gilmore City, Iowa, took her junior year from Sioux Falls College to travel to Japan and study at International Christian University. As she returned she shared with us a few snatches of reflection about her year and the new horizons she experienced:

. . . I think I subconsciously began to accept that people

[1] Incident reported by Secretary for Southeast Asia, United Presbyterian Church.

were going to do far more for me than I could for them, and so all I could do was be me and live and love. . . . I had a great year because of good relationships. . . . Really it's not to ignore differences but to go deeper that is truly satisfying. . . . Hiking club and teaching English were my main activities, in time involvement and satisfaction. . . . I hadn't planned to teach English . . . but there was such a demand for native English speakers. . . . Nearly anyplace someone might come up to me and ask, "May I please speak English with you?" I'd usually agree and met some interesting people that way. . . . I also did some work with the campus bilingual newspaper, belonged to Japan-United States Student Congress, was a member of the ICU Church Mission Committee, and attended a seminar on Becoming Human in the Modern World. . . . I really think getting to know people well and letting them really know me was both my most valuable contribution and most creative activity.

. . . From the example of Japanese students, being asked for my opinion many times, study, getting closer to the action, and knowing many nationalities including more concerned Americans, I have become much more aware of world affairs. . . . I believe in missions which say "I have been blessed and need to share." The institutional Christian Church . . . has the resources to do great good. I have seen it and been proud in Japan, Taiwan, and Hong Kong, where concerned people show it, usually through secular teaching. . . . I saw mission work and knew missionaries, I worshiped with Christians of other races, I saw longing for good and physical need. . . . Christ has made a difference in my response to life. People matter most. Positive living, rather than "do not's" or theory, is important. . . . I cannot lead a middle-class existence of becoming settled, acquiring things, being satisfied; I must be worthwhile.

. . . Really, nothing can prepare one for experiences abroad; just people with the right attitude must be sent.[2]

CONSIDER OTHER INVOLVEMENTS OF PEOPLE OVERSEAS:

1. Christian servicemen among the Seabees in Okinawa constructed a chapel in their spare time, for Okinawan worship.
2. The Union (English language) Church in

[2] From Junior Year Abroad report by Bethene Trexel, quoted by permission.

Tokyo, Japan, financed a telephone ministry to help Japanese people in emergency needs.
3. California Youth Caravan joined Japanese students to build a chapel for a youth camp in northern Japan, with the cost of the chapel met by funds raised in the U.S.A. and Japan.
4. An American doctor and his family paid their way to go to Thailand to spend their vacation with the doctor serving as physician at a small hospital-clinic in the hills so that the missionary doctor there could get away for a three-month furlough.
5. An American engineer went at his own expense to Africa to put in a water pumping system for a mission compound and hospital.
6. Peace Corps young people in the Philippines gave Christian witness as they took part in the Philippine churches.

SUMMARY

What are the values in direct involvement in mission overseas which are possible to youth and laymen today?

What dangers or limitations are there in this program?

Just as we hope as laymen to make a Christian contribution overseas, are there ways in which Asian and African Christians can or do make a contribution to us as they visit the United States?

WORSHIP SUGGESTIONS

Bible verses to ponder:
  Romans 1:16—not ashamed of the gospel
  2 Timothy 1:6—stir up the gift of God in you
  Acts 17:26—He made from one every nation
See the poem "Discovery," in Songs of the Slums, a book of poems by Toyohiko Kagawa (Abingdon Press).
Look up prayers from around the world, The World at One in Prayer, by Daniel Fleming (Harper & Row, Publishers).

THE THIRD-WORLD CHURCH
by RUSSELL E. BROWN

TARGET

To recognize that we can't all go overseas, that some of the biggest tasks in mission cannot be "do-it-yourself" projects in which we are directly involved, but that we need also to give backing and support to the national churches of the developing countries and their indigenous leadership.

INTRODUCTION

Personal experiences in another country can add much to our understanding and make us more committed Christians and church members. But there are also limitations in this direct involvement. For example, on a short visit overseas we usually lack the understanding of language and culture that would make possible a deep level of communication. We are usually limited to the contribution we can make through a specific task, plus the witness of our life.

So if we are to help with a deep and lasting contribution to the spread of Christianity, we must be ready to help support the national churches of those countries and their leaders and the career missionaries who are able to work with them at a depth level.

You might want to show a film or filmstrip in this session illustrating the work your denomination is doing overseas. Or you might want to have a Third-World guest present who could report on the situation of the Christian church in his country.

Advance Preparation Is Needed Here

PLANS

BRAINSTORMING

What do we mean by the terms "the third world" or "the developing nations"?

These terms are attempts to get away from the formerly used term "the underdeveloped nations." This term seemed to be derogatory or judgmental, so someone changed it to "the developing nations." However, this term still seems to be a "put-down," suggesting that we are developed and they are not, or that the basis of deciding the status of a nation is the degree of its use of machinery and Western technology. So the new term for the developing nations and peoples is "third world," with the understanding that the first world would be Europe—North America and the second would be the Soviet bloc countries. Also the Black population within the U.S.A. may refer to themselves as a third-world people.

DISCUSS

A church in New Jersey has provided scholarship funds to help bring third-world Christian leaders for theological studies in the United States. This has brought to the church personal contact with Asian and African churchmen who return to become leaders in their nation. The vestibule of the church, lined with portrait pictures of these leaders, is a wonderful and constant reminder of the world contacts of this church. Could your church find similar contact with third-world church leaders?

54

Other possibilities: Look about in your community to see if there are immigrants from third-world nations living in your midst. Or your church might hold a foreign students' weekend, bringing several overseas students from a nearby city to be guests with you for the weekend.

One church in Michigan had a fine group of Indonesians in their rural community one weekend —all of them in church Sunday morning, even though their own faith was Moslem. They enjoyed a rich experience of international and interfaith sharing. Other churches have developed correspondence with a church in the third world and exchanged pictures and greetings.

Can you think of other ways to make your church's supportive relationship to third-world churches and leaders more vivid?

REPORT

Meet a third-world Christian leader—*Thra Benny Gyaw, of Thailand ("Thra" means teacher or leader).*

When the Thai government began to take an interest in the long neglected mountain people, they hired anthropologists from the West to investigate the life and customs of each tribal group.

Thus, Peter Kunstadter, Ph.D., anthropologist of the University of Washington, arrived in Maesariang, Northern Thailand, assigned by the Thai government to study the Karen people. He is Jewish by race but agnostic in thinking. His wife is a believing, practicing Catholic. He knows both the Jewish and the Christian religious heritage better than most believers.

Because he did not know the Karen language, he sought out a Karen who knew English as his interpreter and found Thra Benny Gyaw. Thra Benny has been a lifelong Christian. Brought up in the church in Burma, he graduated from Judson College in Rangoon and held responsible positions in Burman life until the exigencies of post-war political turmoil landed him in Thailand.

He is an enthusiastic Christian. He and his wife, La Say, manage a boarding house, acting as parents to a family of fifty Karen mountain children who have come down to the town of Maesariang to attend school. Besides this, he is a competent linguist, now engaged in translating the New Testament into the Karen dialect spoken by the mountain people in Thailand. He is a leader of the Karen church, making many evangelistic trips with missionaries and pastors to the isolated villages of his non-Christian brethren.

Anthropologist Peter Kunstadter and Thra Benny quickly developed high mutual regard and personal friendship. They lived in non-Christian Karen villages for weeks at a time while Dr. Kunstadter filled notebooks with his analyses of the life situation of the people. Thra Benny was quick to catch on to the vast value of anthropological analysis, but remained a winsome and caring Christian person. Soon men were gathering for his teaching and prayer meeting early in the morning, while it was

still dark, before they left for the day's work in the mountainside fields.

Of course Benny did not waken Dr. Kunstadter to attend these informal conversations and prayers. When Dr. Kunstadter realized what was happening, he was quite put out with his interpreter and friend because he was not included. Benny said: "You don't want to get up in the night for religious talk and prayer. You don't believe in God. You wouldn't want to come." To which Dr. Kunstadter replied: "What do you mean, I wouldn't want to come? How can I understand these people if I don't know what they are praying about? What these people are praying about could be the most important thing in this village." And so he came, asking Benny to translate the prayers of these new seeking Christians, word for word.

The February, 1972, issue of the *National Geographic* magazine carries the feature story of Dr. Kunstadter's study of the Karens. He describes life in the village of Laykawkey in typical secular-anthropological spirit. He points out the problems as the twentieth-century world presses on this village: population crowding, lack of adequate food supply, the debilitating effects of poor nutrition, primitive agricultural methods, and opium smoking. The anthropologist *can only describe*. But Thra Benny and the Christian church of Thailand *can prescribe*.

From the Christian hospital in Maesariang public health workers are teaching family planning. Christian agriculturalists are introducing better crops and methods. A school is opening. And today the village of Laykawkey has become a Christian village.[1]

SUMMARY

Thra Benny and his fellow Christians have manpower and zeal. They believe that the Christian faith opens the minds of villagers to new ideas, and that linked to Christianity is the hope for better health, better agriculture, and a chance to help Thailand villages to survive. But for this program financial help is needed beyond what the Christians of Thailand can provide, and also medical and agricultural personnel from the American mission group in Thailand is needed to work along with Thai fellow workers. Part of our involvement in world mission can be to give the backing of prayer and financial support to programs of this nature around the world.

WORSHIP

Romans 10:14-15 ". . . unless they are sent."
Ephesians 2:13-18 ". . . he came and preached peace to you who were far off."

[1] Account described by Thra Benny Gyaw to an American Missions Executive.

57

"If a man does not keep pace with his companions, perhaps it is because he hears a different drummer. Let him step to the music which he hears, however measured or far away."

—Henry David Thoreau

HE HEARS A DIFFERENT DRUMMER

by JEAN YOST MAYER

TARGET

To give positive feelings about loners as individuals with offerings to make.

INTRODUCTION

In our culture, where grouping and crowds are given such importance, many tend to have negative thoughts about those who choose to stand apart. When dealing with youth, it is important to remember that the most voices present at any given time may not express the best direction for the program to go. I have seen examples where a youth prefers to teach in the church school rather than participate in a youth group that, to that person, seemed cliquish and superficial. These people may feel they have an offering which is greater than that to which the group will say OK.[1]

In the age of busy-ness that we now live in, it may be necessary to face the division of time problem. Some "loners" (from your perspective) may be busy in other groups such as school, sports, or volunteer work. Such things hold a higher priority for that person. They may also be very worthwhile activities. Mention of accomplishments in outside endeavors in the youth paper or church bulletin might say to that person that he is accepted.

Another possibility is the youth who feels too insecure. "What I am is not good enough." A group can help here, but "rushing" the person with false smiles and handshakes will not do the job. Sincere efforts by sensitive adults and youth will find offerings this person has that make him OK as

[1] This is a reference to Thomas A. Harris' book entitled *I'm OK—You're OK*, published by Harper and Row. It is recommended reading for anyone interested in relationships among people.

he is right now. *It is important not to make a loner feel that change on his part is necessary before the group will "accept" him.*

PLAN

The program is designed to let those in the group, both adult and youth, feel like or identify with one who is alone or seems to stand apart. Preparation consists of reserving a room large enough so that those participating can get away from each other. Newsprint and markers or a blackboard and chalk are also needed.

EXERCISE

1. Tell each person in the group to find a place where he or she can be alone and not look at anyone else. Suggest that they face a wall or corner.

2. Some biblical figures were loners. Abraham obeyed God when asked to leave his home and sojourn in a land of promise. Jacob was alone when he met God and dreamed of a ladder. Moses was alone when he met God at a burning bush. Elijah was alone when he met God as a still small voice. Read about him in 1 Kings 19:10-14. As we are together, yet alone, let us listen to words of others who knew the meaning of being alone: Psalm 69:16-20; Ecclesiastes 4:7-12; and John 16:31-35. Jesus was alone in temptation. He felt alone upon the cross.

3. Ask the group to think of a very lonely moment in each of their lives when they felt like crying or did cry because "nobody cared." (2 minutes)

4. Ask the group to turn to one other person and in twos discuss each person's moment. Be sure

to listen as you expect the other person to listen to you. (8 minutes)

5. Separate yourselves again and think of a time when being alone brought you joy or pleasure, such as listening to a record or tape or walking barefoot in the rain. (2 minutes)

6. Again in twos, tell each other about that experience. (8 minutes)

7. Gather the group around the newsprint or blackboard. If the group numbers more than sixteen, consider two groups with two leaders. Eight to ten is an ideal size. The remainder of this program should take at least thirty minutes. It can continue to the end of your meeting time or as long as feelings and ideas keep coming from the group.

8. Make two columns on the newsprint or blackboard and ask for good and bad feelings about being alone. Notice how the group comes forth with answers. Are good or bad feelings mentioned first? Are people discussing how they *felt* or simply relating facts? "My Mother was late picking me up at the airport (fact), and I was scared (feeling)!" "I spent the day reading in my room (fact) and it was so relaxing (feeling)." Do you feel that people in the group are beginning to look at some good factors in being alone as well as bad ones?

9. Ask the group to share what or who "brought them out" of bad "alone" situations. Does this give any hints as to needs of youth in your church who "don't seem to fit in"? What actions might be taken? After determining action steps, be sure that plans are made to delegate action. (The plans should be discussed only if the "loners" are not present.) Some might include:
   a. Ask the pastor for a program spot at a church dinner or other appropriate time where a loner poet might read some original poetry and/or someone who plays a guitar or other instrument may perform. Why not ask whoever plans these programs regularly to invite the loner to participate?
   b. Check with the church school superintendent to see if any young loners might be suited for work in the church school. Make sure they are included in teachers' meetings and not considered "only helpers who don't have time to come to meetings."
   c. Does your church tape the sermon for shut-ins? Could your "electronics loner" do this?
   d. Could going to a state or national conference be a help to "open up" the youth who needs a broader scope to relate to?
   e. Does your church need someone to build or repair so the kid with the hammer-and-saw-love has something to do?

The most important factor is a sincere appreciation of what the loner feels about his or her situation. The adults' attitude of acceptance or a feeling that the youth is OK is most important. The "Why don't you join us on Sunday night?" as you pass in the hall or on the street does not give the loner a chance to tell you what he or she is all about. The telephone committee can be your worst enemy. It can be impersonal and allows a person to say "no" too easily. Are your callers dedicated to bringing more young people to realization of individual worth? Is the group using the fact that "everybody got a call" to exclude some who are harder to get to know?

Another factor is that some people never "join." This situation calls for a different kind of ministry —the one-to-one conversation where you listen and assure the individual that he or she is OK.

YOU CAN MAKE A DIFFERENCE
by ROBERT B. WALLACE

PURPOSE

This is the first of two meetings designed to help your youth group develop a sense of responsibility for the community in which you live and to develop skills for helping to bring about change. The first session will help you focus on a particular concern, and the second will give you an opportunity to try your skills in making a difference in your town.

Jesus represents the crossing point of man and God, and he reminds us that God is to be met at the place where we take human need seriously; but we can best serve others when we look at their needs in the light of Christ.

Remember your chemistry? A "catalyst" is an element which enables a reaction to take place. The Christian is called to be a catalyst. That means he is not to get the spotlight and draw attention to himself (and his youth group) but is to be the one who gets things started, brings the right people together, asks the big question, and then moves into the background. Another term is "change agent." The Christian needs to know that he can help catalyze change. He or she can make a difference!

PREPARATION

Advance Preparation

Have a small planning group prepare the first meeting which will attempt to pinpoint: (1) What are the major social problems in your town? (2) Which of these can youth best speak to? (3) Which one of these do you feel is most crucial at this time?

Supplies Needed

Arrange for several persons to serve on a panel. Invite one or two political leaders in your community, two youth from another church (remember you don't want to do this alone if you are really concerned about others), and select one of your group to moderate.

Have newsprint on the wall with markers and small cards and pencils ready.

PROGRAM

1. Open with a brief worship experience in which you list the changes that Jesus helped bring about in his world. Portray him as a "change agent." Show how he was a catalyst to change in Zacchaeus (Luke 19:1-10) and the woman at the well (John 4:7-42). Introduce the program by explaining that the goal is to help us decide our responsibility as Christians for our town.

2. Have each person in the group write on a card the major problems in your town. If help is needed for this task, you might mention the following areas of concern: political life, how decisions are made, who has the power (who does not), recreation opportunities, crime control, use of public land and property, pollution control, needs of the poor, and street repair.

3. Collect the cards and write the problems on the newsprint.

4. Ask the panel to respond to the listing and discuss:
   - What do they think are the major problems?
   - Which of these problems can youth be most effective in solving?

5. Ask the total group to choose one area of concern for your focus. Use this formula to decide which is the right one for you.

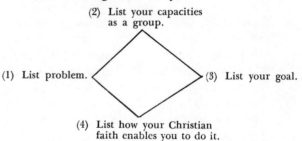

(2) List your capacities as a group.

(1) List problem.   (3) List your goal.

(4) List how your Christian faith enables you to do it.

Some diamonds will look like this because they are long on problem but short on goal. Another will look like this because the group simply doesn't have the capacity to handle it. If this is the case with you, then focus on a problem where you have more capacity. But be careful. Don't underrate yourselves!

6. Ask for volunteers to work on developing a strategy for your task.

STRATEGIES FOR CHANGE
by ROBERT B. WALLACE

PURPOSE

To help the group see that, no matter how small, it can be a catalyst or change agent. To be effective as a change agent you need:

1. A support community. You can't do the job alone, and someone needs to keep giving you courage and Christian perspective.

2. To have a clear objective and strategy (specific steps), so as not to be victimized by all the temptations to compromise.

3. To enable others to do the job and take responsibility.

Possibly you will want to put these points on the board for the meeting.

PREPARATION

Advance Preparation

A task force should meet at least once to list objectives along with negative forces (that will work against your goal) and positive forces (help you can count on). The task force should also decide some strategy (how we'll provide a support group and who are possible allies in working on the problem).

Have someone else plan the actual meeting (the task force will have enough to do).

PROGRAM

1. Have the task group report and give its list of objectives and strategies.

2. Play a game in which everyone in the group (except the task force) acts out a scene portraying one or more persons who have decided to be change agents attempting to bring about change. For example: If the problem is the quality of movies, stage a meeting of the Chamber of Commerce. Have someone be a chamber member with whom the youth have spoken and another be a young person who is attending the meeting. Have the remaining people represent the negative forces you have listed. Role-play a discussion.

   Ask the task force to be critics who will watch for:
   - What kind of support was given to those who sought to bring about change?
   - Were the objectives clear?
   - Did the change agent enable people or did he seek to do it himself?

3. Ask for group response and review how you will go about actively influencing change. Select persons to be the change agents in your group and ask the task force to monitor the project and report back in three weeks.

4. Close with prayer for those who will be your change agents.

VANDALISM
by JOHN ANDRE

INTRODUCTION

Recently, in a small midwestern town, two boys walked up to a parking meter during the day and began shaking it until it came loose from the ground. Later, a car was bombarded with eggs. Vandalism!

Why do people commit acts of vandalism? Is it a form of rebellion? Are they just mean? Why do they want to damage another person's property? Is it actually an attempt to hurt the person through their property?

Many times the real motivation is suppressed hostility towards a world that has demanded conformity. This is one way in which the person is able to release his hostility.

We all experience suppression in our lives from outside forces. We must find ways of releasing the negative feelings which come from being suppressed. Acts of vandalism are the result of misdirected hostility.

The youth group of a church can be helpful by discussing ways of releasing hostile feelings. Helping youth find constructive ways of releasing their hostile feelings can be more beneficial than moralizing on the "no-nos" of acts of vandalism. While destruction of property cannot be condoned, we must ultimately help each other find more constructive ways of releasing feelings.

PROCESS

DEFINITIONS AND FINGER PAINTING

Introduce the topic for the meeting by having the group members write a definition of vandalism. They should then be given finger painting supplies and put in groups of two or three. Each group is to work together to make a painting that illustrates their feelings about vandalism. Give them approximately twenty minutes to finish.

As a total group share the meanings of the paintings and discuss the following questions: What constitutes an act of vandalism? Share your experience from any time you have felt like doing an act of vandalism. What did you do with your feelings? This is primarily an opportunity to gather data, not an opportunity to moralize.

DRAMA

If you prefer, drama can be used to discover the feelings of the vandal and the victim. Divide the group in half. One group is to play the role of vandals and discuss how they felt breaking the windows of a homeowner. The other group should select a couple to play the role of the homeowners, and the rest of that group would play their neighbors. In the second role play, have a homeowner discuss with his neighbors how he felt when he found his home vandalized.

DISCUSSION

Following either option, a discussion should follow of ways in which hostility can be released in constructive ways. Examples of hostility being released constructively are: beating a pillow until exhausted, playing tennis, etc.

Discuss ways to identify the real sources of hostility in the lives of youth and help them design ways to resolve their hostility at the source. Perhaps through a meaningful dialogue the feelings of hostility can be resolved constructively.

WORSHIP

Have someone in the group read 1 Corinthians 13 and conclude by having the group share any feelings they now have. Finally, sing or listen to the record "Bridge over Troubled Waters."

POSITIVE STEPS TO NARROW THE GENERATION CHASM

by SHARON BALLENGER and KATHLEEN SPENCER

Supplies needed

TARGET

To come to a realistic understanding of my role in the family and to explore some new ways of relating to family members.

LEADER'S PREPARATION

Bring paper and pencils, felt-tip pens, crayons; a 2' x 4' piece of wood; a 3-D or small jigsaw puzzle; Bibles.

Read the program and Bible verses before the meeting. *Adapt* the activities to your own group and facilities. *Relax,* have fun, let the group do the talking.

INTRODUCTION

Attention! Sit up straight, chin up, shoulders back, minds alert. Surprise! We're going to participate in a program relating to families. Probably never in the history of the whole world have there been so many articles, TV shows, books, sermons, institutes, symposiums, class sessions, and town meetings dealing in, around, and about the *family.* We've run the gamut from wringing our hands wondering if Dad really should be the head of the family or the opposite end! All of this concern addresses itself to the disturbing question, "Should families as we know them today even exist?" My, that is a frightening thought!

Well, relax. Studies show that most people still believe in the family structure, and homes, and real live LOVE. Therefore, this program deals with YOU as a family member—how you fit in with Mom, Dad, brothers, sisters—how you see conflicts in the home—and explores more effective ways of BEING a family member.

PLANS

PART ONE

The following ideas are designed to encourage discussion within your youth group. Choose one or two that seem the most suited to your group members and go on from there.

In Scripture

Have a member structure a model of his family using other group members. Show how each person in the family relates to the others. EXAMPLE: Mom and Dad are close so they stand close together. But brother "A" and Dad don't get along, so brother "A" stands by mother far away from father. But I am closest of all of the kids to my Mom, so I stand between my Mom and brother "A". Any group member who wishes to share his family structure in this FAMILY SCULPT should do so; the group should ask questions and make observations.

In Quiet Words

Depending on the closeness of your group, take time to share and relate the following:
- A time you felt close to Mom/Dad.
- Describe a big fight you've had with a family member and how it was resolved.
- Describe one parent as if he or she were not related to you, i.e., as an individual, a person, and not a parent.

DISCUSS FEELINGS

Have group members mill about the room. At the signal "back to back" they are to select a partner and stand back to back with that person. If there is an extra person the leader participates. When all have partners, the first topic below is stated. At the signal "face to face," couples turn around and discuss the given topic for three minutes. After the time is over, the leader announces "back to back." New groups of twos are formed standing back to back. The second topic for discussion is given, and at the command "face to face" the second topic is discussed. All four topics are to be used in this way. An opportunity should be provided for the whole group to share insights from the discussions. Here are the topics to be used:
- This is how I get my way (in my family).
- This is one way I share feelings.

- This is how I fight.
- This is one way I show love.

PART TWO

These activities give the group a chance to experience and examine emotions that are felt in the family group. Do as many as possible.

On Trust

Have the group divide into twos and alternate leading each other blindfolded around the room. Discuss trusting relationships. How am I accepted in my family? In what way do I show acceptance of other family members? Whom do I trust most in my family?

On Fear

Have each member walk blindfolded (or with eyes closed) on the edge of a 2′ x 4′ piece of wood. Discuss fear of the unknown, fear of things which you don't understand. What are my fears? Is my family aware of my fears? What fears do I see expressed by Mom/Dad? Can I help alleviate any of these?

On Pressure

Have each member try to assemble a puzzle (3-D or jigsaw) in thirty seconds. Discuss experiencing pressures in the family. Is there pressure to compete or conform in my family? How do pressures on me from my school and my friends cause conflicts in the family?

Creative Expression and Worship

THINK TANK

In the next few minutes, based on the discoveries you've made regarding your present role in your family, brainstorm with other group members some possible new ways of relating to family members in the coming weeks. Be inventive. Don't criticize anyone's idea. Jot down those ideas you may be able to use. Try for positive, refreshing, *loving, communicative* means for relating to family members. Determine to try at least one realistic method. Perhaps a follow-up meeting could be used so that group members can share their experiences.

Some ideas that may bob up are: "I will try to ask for and listen to my parents' opinions." "I will urge my folks to share their feelings with me." "I will try to see my family as a group of individuals who love each other."

Read, then paraphrase, these Bible passages relating them to your family experiences:

James 3:1-5

Luke 2:41-49

Luke 15:20

> REMEMBER: A generation chasm is as painful for parents as it is for you. But only your desire to change the conditions with others will reverse or alter the status quo.

WRAP UP

Have each member express his thoughts about the hour with crayons, felt-tip pens, or even words. Here's a sample thought which may help to provoke expressions on what has happened in the group:

After we talked about trust, I felt creepy. I realized my Mom doesn't want to talk to me because I never talk to her anymore, or I yell, if I say anything at all. I don't know why I do it. But I can see now I feel put down when Mom disagrees with my ideas. I bet she doesn't realize how much she hurts me. This discussion has told me that if I talk more with Mom she may come to understand me better, and therefore she wouldn't disagree with me so much. I'm scared to try, but I don't like all the fighting I've experienced.

SOME NEW EXPRESSIONS OF SOME OLD WORDS: "I DO!"

by ROBERT A. NOBLETT

INTRODUCTION

If you have been reading the daily papers or the weekly news magazines lately, you've undoubtedly noticed that more and more attention is being focused on the new marriage styles. People are asking whether marriage, as presently constituted, is as meaningful and viable as it is meant to be. In short, is it working?

When speaking of the causes that have given rise to the new styles of marriage, it might be helpful to think in terms of an old law of physical science: For every action, there is an opposite and equal reaction. Further, when we think of action and reaction, we think of extremes. And that is precisely the reason why many new forms of marriage have emerged. There has been, in many cases, justifiable dissatisfaction with marriage as it has been "normally" constituted. Extreme cases of insensitivity and unfairness have caused some to throw out the baby with the bath water and in turn, embrace forms of married life that are a far cry from those originally practiced.

Before going a step further, we ought to say what we mean by new marriage styles! They refer to a whole cluster of new arrangements which vary significantly from marriage as it is commonly viewed and practiced in American culture and which include the following forms: (1) role reversals, where husband and wife may exchange culturally accepted and expected roles (the wife may become the breadwinner and the husband the homemaker); (2) trial marriages and contractual arrangements, whereby a couple agree to live together for a specific period of time, at the end of which they decide whether or not to continue; (3) communes, where many families live together and share "family" responsibilities, such as food preparation and child care, forming what is called an "extended" family; (4) single parent families; and (5) trio or larger group marriages.

PLANS

EXPRESSING FEELINGS

To break open the conversation about the present disenchantment with the "typical" marriage, have the group reveal the kinds of feelings they have about contemporary marriage. What is good about it? What may be lacking in it?

While the group members will not have experienced marriage firsthand, they do live in families and daily observe their parents. Moreover, they have exposure to other married couples through school, church, and family friends.

Record these feelings on newsprint. As a way of getting people moving, the leader might refer to two TV "families" that represent opposite extremes and ask for a critical evaluation of both. This approach would enable the conversation to begin on common ground and also pave the way for the introduction of more personal feelings. No one is apt to jump in right away and spill deep feelings about the marriage of people close to him or her.

The feelings will obviously reflect the experience and perceptions of the group members. Some will feel marriage to be exciting, fulfilling, and meaningful, and others will feel it to be inhibitive, intolerable, dull, and dehumanizing. Those who have embraced the new marriage styles, of course, fall into the latter camp. But negative feelings do not just occur. There are reasons for them. Have the group members then focus their attention on the reasons why people have negative feelings which have led to the creation of the variant styles.

As a way of introducing some affirmative input in the midst of a critical debate on marriage, the group might enjoy some readings from Lois Wyse, who has written several books of poems for married people. (Check your local library.) Her books are most insightful and offer a glimpse of married life in full bloom.

EVALUATION

Now evaluate, from the perspective of the Christian faith, the new marriage styles. It would be counterproductive to simply criticize, so think of those tenets of the new marriage styles that would enhance the Christian understanding of marriage.

BIBLE STUDY

The prior question, of course, is what is the Christian understanding of marriage? The roots of the Christian position are to be found in biblical faith, where the rightness and honor of the institution are strongly affirmed. The picture we receive is that marriage is natural and healthy and to be encouraged. ". . . a man shall leave his father and mother, and be made one with his wife; and the two shall become one flesh" (Mark 10:7, NEB). Moreover, it is an intimate relationship and one which the Bible uses to define God's relationship with us. It was created by God for the fulfillment of men and women. Through the marriage relationship, a man and a woman are able to experience life's deepest meaning and significance. Marriage affords two people the experience of understanding what it means to create and to nurture and to grow in affection.

COMPARISON

Recall now your discussions about new marriage styles and list those practices in the new styles which you feel would enhance the Christian understanding of marriage.

In an attempt to test out your conclusions about the new marriage styles, consider inviting three or four couples from your church who would be willing to discuss, openly and against the backdrop of their marriages, the new styles. Or, invite persons practicing these new styles of marriage. Ask them how they view their marriages in light of religious faith and what contributions they feel the new marital variations could make to Christian marriage. In fairness to both the couples and the program, these people should be contacted far enough in advance so that they can prepare adequately.

WRITING A MARRIAGE CONTRACT

As an alternative or a further feature of this meeting, have the participants draft their own marriage ceremonies, keeping in mind the many issues that have been raised since the beginning of their conversations about the new styles in marriage. Have them pay particular attention to the content of the vows they would make to their "unknown" husband/wife. Again, the wider parish might be interested in your conclusions, and those conclusions could be presented via these written ceremonies which could be published in the church newsletter.

Whatever conclusions you may reach, always keep in mind that marriage at its best is a relationship which is meant to make it possible for a man and a woman to walk, as Peter Marshall termed them, "the halls of highest human happiness!"

IS MARRIAGE A SOMETIMES THING?
by ROBERT A. NOBLETT

INTRODUCTION

We would be remiss if we assumed that those who have advocated the new marriage styles were in toto a group of malcontents who had nothing better to do other than raise havoc with a perfectly good institution. The fact that one marriage in four ends in divorce is a sobering statistic. The question before us then is this: What can we learn from the debate? Or, what are the legitimate issues that deserve a hearing?

PLAN

COMMITTEE RESEARCH

Ask the group to think of themselves as a committee appointed to investigate and then report back on new marriage styles. There has been much conversation in the community about this matter, and community leaders are concerned that the public debate be harnessed and used for constructive ends. This committee, then, will divide itself up into smaller groupings, each of which will research one of the questions that is going to be the subject of debate. After meeting separately, the group will return and in round-table fashion will give its report on the question it researched. Its "report" may take any form desired. Perhaps it will be verbal; perhaps it will be a role-playing situation; an art form could be used—music, a drawing, a collage.

Write each of the questions and the material under it on separate sheets of paper and give one to each of the small groups.

Here are the questions:

1. What Are We to Make of Mama?

Whenever we read of new marriage styles, we soon hear of the feminist movement. Women's liberation has had much to say about what marriage ought and ought not mean for women.

In the late fifties, there was a weekly television program entitled "I Remember Mama." Mama was a placid person, almost part of the home furnishings. But she has come a long way since then! Reacting to the continual rebuffs of male chauvinism and affirming her rightful place in the scheme of things, the American mother has experienced a revolution in her role. Now the talk is of day-care centers, women's rightful place in the business community, and female participation in the political process.

The tragedy of the situation is that those at opposite poles of opinion have unproductively attacked each other. Those who choose to remain housewives are deemed victims of male dominance, and those who choose careers and children are deemed irresponsible parents.

The question now is: What value can be derived from both stances, and is it possible that in sifting from both, a "new woman" can emerge? Bat this one about. What would you say constitutes the "new married womanhood"? Is it children and vocation, or is it children versus vocation? What is her "wifely" role? What of her community role? Keep in mind that you are to give a report which highlights the values of the debate.

Study of and reaction to the following Scripture passages may be helpful: Proverbs 31:10-31; 1 Timothy 2:8-15; 2 Timothy 3:16.

2. Is Marriage a Sometimes Thing?

Another theme that can be heard in the debate over new marriage styles is that of marital success and failure. There are those that advocate a trial period in a marriage that will allow the participants time to see if a marriage in fact can be created. While some may find the tactic questionable, there can surely be no one who can find the intent objectionable. More should pursue their marriages with seriousness and intentionality! Here is where the crunch comes: Is it possible for a deep marriage to develop within a context where every marital act is carried out under the banner of temporariness, or is it apt to do the very thing it is trying to avoid—provide a rationale for holding back the gut commitment that is indispensable to the growth of a marriage? In other words, if the whole thing is a kind of adult version of "playing house," might the participants be prone to hold back their total inner selves either out of laxity or the fear that the

partner may get frustrated (as indeed everyone gets frustrated in marriage) and use the trial arrangement as a way of easing out of his or her responsibility? These are some of the issues this group should raise.

3. How About Papa?

The conversation and activity about women's liberation has automatically forced us to rethink the role of the male in marriage and the family as well. What about Papa? Traditionally he has been breadwinner and monarch of his home. But now people are asking if both man and wife have been robbed of the fullness of familial experience by being "assigned" to traditional roles.

Since the wife/mother is being discussed in another group, let us zero in on Dad and raise the following questions: For practical reasons (Mother is home more than Dad and is usually more versed in culinary arts) women usually assume greater responsibility for the rearing of children, but could it be that this is even a greater reason for Dad, when he is home, to spend time with and share responsibility for his children? The fact of the matter is, the loss is his, should he neglect to do so. Moreover, might Dad understand more fully his wife's role and perhaps free her for other equally important undertakings (community involvement, reading, etc.), if on frequent occasions he assumed some of the domestic chores such as cleaning, cooking, and food shopping? Further, will it not enhance the solidarity of the family if husband and wife (and, when appropriate, children) share together in decisions (financial, social, recreational) which affect the entire family?

In one recently publicized situation, the husband was in a position to free himself from one day of work per week, and assume full domestic responsibility. While this would not be possible in a majority of cases, should the father and husband see his family responsibilities extending far beyond the workaday world?

Study of and reaction to the following Scripture passage may be helpful: Ephesians 5:21-33. Consider the significance of Jesus' name for God, "Father."

4. How Extended Should the Family Be?

The term "extended family" means a situation where a family of mother, father, and children has ties beyond itself. These may be with relatives or friends. This idea has been the driving force behind the establishment of many communes which bring together people of more than one family unit.

The American experience in the recent past has largely been with the nuclear family. This has especially been the case since the era of widespread mobility during which families have spread across the land, or for that matter, the globe. But now people are asking if there is not benefit, especially for children, in having family relationships with people across the age span.

Consider these issues: Can the nuclear family become too ingrown? What can this lead to? Further, what steps can a family take to make their children, and even mother and father, feel more at home in the world?

Study the following Scripture passages and react to them: Genesis 2:24; Matthew 19:5-6; 2 Timothy 1:5; 3:14-15.

REPORTS

When the tasks have been completed in the subgroups, gather as a total group to hear the reports. This should lead to a general discussion of the issues involved.

WORSHIP SUGGESTIONS

Stand in a circle and join hands. Ask one person to lead in prayer, pausing after each sentence so that the group has time for silent reflection and prayer.

Prayer suggestion: Let us thank God for all the ways in which he has blessed us. (Pause.) Let us thank God for our homes, the love of parents, and others in the home. (Pause.) Let us thank God for our Christian faith and for its meaning. (Pause.) Help us, O God, to develop as whole persons today so that we will have a meaningful marriage tomorrow. (Pause.) Help us to be wise in our dating relationships today that they might be a good basis for a marriage relationship in the future. (Pause.) In Jesus' name. Amen.

SO WHAT'S NEW?

by HAROLD D. MOORE

PURPOSE

To discover how the roles of ministers today are changing and to learn what is new and challenging about those changes.

INTRODUCTION

A minister who was about to retire after a long and effective ministry was recently heard to say, "The ministry has changed more in the last five years than it did in all the other years of my work."

The roles of ministers are changing. Changes are largely dictated by the rapid acceleration of change that we all experience in our culture. The minister who tries to respond to the needs of the people must constantly adjust his or her way of working in order to have an effective ministry.

The minister has long been identified with certain roles in the life of the church and community. Preaching, leading in worship, officiating at weddings or funerals, offering prayer on public occasions are the more visible roles of the minister. Changes in these roles are rather easily seen when they occur.

Ministers experience the greatest change in the less visible roles. The stress which people are experiencing puts increasing demands on the minister for greater skills and services. Personal and family difficulties require the minister to be an effective counselor. Skills in resolving conflict are needed more and more. As institutions grow more complex and experience greater stress, the need for understanding how organizations develop and function becomes more important.

Most ministers find they need skill in the areas of interpersonal relationships and group work. These are the areas for which they feel least equipped by their formal training. Many ministers engage in continuing education as a means of upgrading their skills and effectiveness.

An important part of any ministry is the relationship between the minister and the people he or she serves. One of the real factors in the changing role of the minister is the difference in the ideas of ministers and lay people. Many congregations experience differences in theology, social issues, the mission of the church, or the way it should conduct its worship. Ways of dealing creatively with these tensions often result in changing roles for the minister.

One of the best ways to understand the changing role of the minister is to ask some ministers what their experience is. Our plans for this meeting suggest three ways of doing that. Choose the plan that seems most appropriate for your group.

PLAN ONE

Invite two ministers to come as guests to your meeting, one minister who is near retirement age and another who has just started in the ministry.

Instead of having them speak to the topic of changes in the ministry, arrange the program so you can find out from them what you want to know.

One way to do this is to arrange the format like a TV "Meet the Press" interview. (If you have videotape equipment or movie equipment, you may want to film the "show" in advance.) Select three or four youth to be the interviewing panel and have them ask questions of the guest ministers. The focus of the questions should be something like this:

1. How do they see the role of the minister today?
2. How has the older minister experienced changes in the work of ministry over the years?
3. How does the younger minister anticipate the role of ministers to change in the years to come?

After the simulated TV discussion has been concluded, ask the entire group to sum up what they heard. Ask what things seem promising, hopeful, and even exciting about the changes that are taking place in the ministry.

PLAN TWO

Sometimes ministers are not available at a specific time. If that is the case, have one person interview an older minister and another person interview a younger minister. Have their interviews take the same focus as the interviews in

Plan One. Then have the two interviewers play the role of the younger minister and the older minister, following the same format of Plan One.

PLAN THREE

A third option is to show the 15-minute movie *Making a Difference*. This is a film of three ministers talking about their work. (This movie may be available from your denominational film library. If they do not have it, they can probably tell you where you may obtain it.)

The effective use of a film requires a great deal of preparation on the part of the presenter. A guide for the use of the film accompanies it.

WORSHIP

Scripture: Luke 4:1-15
Meditation

A brief meditation might point out how the temptations of Jesus presented three distinct roles for ministry. Verses 3 and 4 present the temptation to meet only the physical needs of people. Verses 5 and 6 present the temptation to minister to the needs of people through political power. Verses 9 to 11 present the temptation to leave the responsibility of ministry up to God. Jesus rejected all of these roles and accepted the role of a servant.

Scripture: Philippians 2:5-11
Prayer

WHO, ME?

by HAROLD D. MOORE

PURPOSE

To help the group members think about the Christian ministry and consider it as a viable choice for their life and work.

INTRODUCTION

One of the most important choices you will ever make is the choice of a life work. Some people allow themselves to simply drift into an occupation. Others take time to make a thoughtful choice about how they will invest their lives.

The world of work holds up a bewildering array of occupational possibilities for the young person. Literally thousands of occupations are available from which to choose. The Christian ministry is but one choice among these countless others. Not everyone can or should be a minister. It is an option, however, that deserves our careful consideration.

There was a time when the word "ministry" would bring to mind only the thought of a pastor in a local church and the activities which made up his or her work. It is not unusual today to think of a number of other kinds of ministry. Ministers serve as chaplains in hospitals, penal institutions, and the armed forces. They serve as college and university pastors. They work as ministers of music and education. Urban ministries, counseling ministries, administrative ministries, and a number of others could be added to this list.

A wide variety of professional people also find a ministry in church-related occupations. Serving as non-ordained, sometimes commissioned personnel, these persons render invaluable service to the Christian cause. Doctors, nurses, social workers, business administrators, and many others are a vital part of the professional leadership ranks of the church.

If you like to work with people in a service profession and want to do so as part of the work of the church, some form of Christian ministry may be for you. Strength of character, dedication, and a willingness to prepare oneself for service are all essential qualities for the consideration of a church-related occupation.

The basic educational requirements for serving as an ordained minister are a four-year college degree and a three-year seminary degree. In addition to this, certain specialized training may be necessary. For those who work in the non-ordained professions, the basic requirements of their profession must be met, plus some seminary training.

Many people in church-related ministries find great satisfaction in their work through being able to respond to the needs of people. To be able to do that, in the name of Christ, is a great privilege.

73

PREPARATION

You will need a chalkboard or some newsprint and marking pens for this session. Be sure to have these ready to go before the time of your meeting. You will need to ask one or two people to help you as described in the process below.

THE PROCESS

1. Begin the meeting by asking the members of the group to report aloud what word first comes to mind when you say the word "ministry." Have one or two people ready to write these words on the chalkboard or newsprint just as quickly as words are suggested. Allow this to go for as long as words are being suggested. Words like "preach," "help," "serve," will probably be among those listed.

2. When the responses of the group have been recorded, state the purpose of the session and share some or all of the introductory material. You may want to talk to your minister in advance of the session and add some of his or her thoughts about the ministry.

3. Divide into groups of three or four persons to discuss these questions:

- What do you find personally appealing about the ministry?
- What would you find personally difficult about the ministry?

Allow ample time for the members of the groups to engage each other at a serious level.

4. Reconvene the group for a report-back of what was significant in the small-group discussions. You might want to put these on the chalkboard or newsprint for further discussion.

WORSHIP

Opening: A letterhead of one of the major denominations carries the sentence, "Where a line representing my talent crosses a line representing the world's need . . . there is God's call for me."

Hymn: "Take My Life and Let It Be"
Scripture Reading: Matthew 25:31-40
Prayer: Ask for God's guidance in the choice of a life work.
Hymn: "O Master, Let Me Walk with Thee"

Resource Suggestion: You may wish to write your denominational headquarters for material on church occupations. "A Listing of Church Occupations" is a valuable summary description of fifty church-related occupations and the educational requirements for each. This listing is available from The Department of Ministry, National Council of Churches of Christ in the U.S.A., 475 Riverside Drive, New York, New York 10027.

74

WHAT'S A PERSON TO DO?

by DONALD R. RASMUSSEN

INTRODUCTION

A most crucial decision that youth have to make is their choice of a vocation.

Since the Reformation, attitudes about the relationship between faith and work have been somewhat disordered. We spoke of "full-time Christian service," meaning church related occupations, thereby implying that faith is somehow compartmentalized. More recently, however, the trend has been to emphasize that every Christian is in "full-time Christian service" no matter what his job may be.

With this in mind, it is particularly important that the church aid students in the important decision about their life work, and here's how to do it!

PLANS

A good way to introduce the subject to your youth might be to use a film or develop a "happening" that will get them thinking about the world of work. A particularly useful film is *Revelation Now* (Family Films) which is free of "talk" but yet gets youth to think about and be able to identify some feelings of anticipation, confusion, frustration, etc.

After the film, have the youth list their feelings and talk about how they empathize with the young man in the film. Writing these feelings down will help them to be seen as positive forces in decision-making as the program progresses.

SCRIPTURE INPUT

Have the group check out such passages as Genesis 1:28; Hebrews 11:8; Ephesians 4:1; 1 Corinthians 7:17. A study of these will lead to a discussion of what is meant by "call."

There is more to choosing a career than sitting around and hoping that lightning will strike or a voice will speak. Even when it seems as though the "light dawns suddenly," analysis often shows

that there has been considerable discovering, praying, planning, and exploring beforehand. Normally the "call" comes quietly, when we have discovered all that we can by use of the mind God has given.

TWO GUIDES

Most of the preceding may sound quite ethereal to youth and not really down to the nuts and bolts of the matter. The question they have is: "How can I discover what I should do in life?" Of course there is no simple answer; if there were, guidance counselors would be out of business. But there are guides that a young person can use to find his way through the maze of occupational choice—guides that can make the discovery process less rough and threatening. Discuss these guides with your group.

1. Discover the Needs of the World

If there is anything that Jesus tried to impress on his followers, it was that they were to be about ministry to the world. In the parable of the good Samaritan, Jesus applauds the unhesitating service given by the Samaritan. Again in Matthew 25 the righteous are inheritors of the kingdom because they fed the hungry, gave drink to the thirsty, welcomed the strangers, clothed the naked, and visited the sick and those in prison. So we find that the needs of our fellow humans become a part of God's "call."

At this point it may be helpful to have the youth list (on chalkboard or newsprint) as many of the world's needs as they can. Such conditions as physical and mental illness, poverty, nutritional starvation, illiteracy, and the need to spread the gospel may be mentioned. This exercise will help youth to begin thinking in terms of a healthy Christian activism about their vocational choice.

2. Discover Yourself

If a Christian is ever to be of help in and to the world he must first know himself. It is more diffi-

75

cult to know one's self. The needs of the world are readily apparent, but knowing one's gifts requires definition and evaluation.

Have the youth divide up into triads (groups of three) and assume the following roles: speaker, responder, and observer. The speaker tells the responder the positive things he sees in the responder's personality and the types of employment in which he or she can envision the responder. The responder may ask questions only for clarification of what the speaker has said. At the end of three minutes the observer takes a few seconds to report what he feels has been going on, and then chairs and roles are switched until all have had an opportunity to understand their personalities as perceived by others.

GUEST COUNSELOR

Advance Preparation Needed

Most school guidance departments are happy and anxious to cooperate with a church in a program such as this and are willing to send a guidance counselor to participate. At this time, the counselor can help the youth understand the following terms and how an analysis of them can be helpful in determining occupational choice: personality; interests; aptitude; ability; achievement. The counselor should point out the standardized tests which evaluate those categories and give some clue as to how these instruments can aid the student in a vocational choice. The counselor should be careful to point out that tests are not foolproof and are to be used only as guides.

Your guest school guidance counselor should have access to a variety of good books and other resources which would be helpful.

Following are some areas of concern you may want to ask your guest leader to deal with: How valid is the "Protestant work ethic" which claims that all legitimate work has dignity? What are occupation trends today? What occupations are now overcrowded? What occupations are anticipated to be overcrowded? There are 40,000 different jobs available in the U.S. today. How can I become familiar with more of them? What is the relationship between life-style and occupational choice? In our changing society how can I prepare so I can be vocationally flexible?

NOTE

Youth advisors are aware that this is one "program" that will continue for several years, and they should make an effort to be supportive as young people struggle through their questions and concerns relating to vocational choice.

RESOURCES

FILMS

Adventures of an *—a ten-minute, color animation—tells the story of life and opens the way for a discussion on the workaday routine.

Mr. Gray—this ten-minute color film illustrates how the day by day routine can imprison unless there is a deeper meaning in life.

Revelation Now—twelve minutes, color—helps youth confront the trauma of growing up as they make decisions and search for meaning.

FILMSTRIPS

If you are unable to get a guidance counselor to come as a guest, quite often your school guidance department will be happy to give you some resources to help you do the job.

Testing, Testing, Testing Part II—a fifteen-minute sound, color filmstrip useful in understanding the place of standardized tests (published by Guidance Associates).

BOOKS

Occupational Literature by Gertrude Forrester—lists places youth can write to get inexpensive or free literature on almost any occupation. Probably available from any public and/or school guidance library.

Occupational Outlook Handbook—a U.S. Government publication which gives growth and trend information for occupational groups telling the nature of the work, employment outlook, etc.

You and Your Lifework—A Christian Choice for Youth by Science Research Associates, Inc. —a way to help youth plan for their careers on the basis of faith.

The Dictionary of Occupational Titles—would be especially helpful for juniors and seniors.

Encyclopedia of Careers—a two-volume set on careers and occupational guidance covering 71 major career fields and 650 occupations (Chicago: J. G. Ferguson Publishing Co.).

The California Occupational Preference Survey — a useful vocational interest inventory.

CREATIONS AND CREATORS

by GEORGE A. LAWSON and RHODA LAWSON BARBER

PURPOSE

To prompt individual reflection through group discussion of literature and poetry.

SETTING

This meeting should take place in comfortable surroundings, such as a living room or church lounge. Seating should be circular. On the wall post art prints and short quotations that illustrate life experiences, such as prints you've selected from the art department of the public library and large-print quotes you've copied from the Bible, from *Speakers' Resources from Contemporary Literature* by Charles L. Wallis, or from other sources. Examples:

1. An excerpt from the creation story in Genesis 1 and 2.
2. From Sinclair Lewis' *Babbitt:* "Thus it came to him merely to run away was folly, because he could never run away from himself."[1]

Obtain copies of the poem "We Are Transmitters" from the book *The Complete Poems of D. H. Lawrence,* edited by Vivian de Sola Pinto and F. Warren Roberts (New York: The Viking Press, Inc., 1964). One copy will do, but several copies would be helpful.

[1] Sinclair Lewis, *Babbitt,* Signet Classic Edition (New York: Harcourt Brace Jovanovich, Inc., 1922, renewed 1950), p. 242. © by Sinclair Lewis. Reprinted by permission of the publisher.

INTRODUCTION

This meeting should begin with a few statements about religion and the arts. Here are some ideas:

When the Bible tells us that man was made in the image of God, it means that, like God, we are also creators. Animals make nests and dams as necessities of life, but man, like God, can create spontaneously and joyously. The arts are creations of man. They tell us something about the man or woman who created them, something about all human beings, and something about God, who is the supreme Creator.

PROCESS

ART WALK

Ask the group to walk around the room, looking at the art prints and quotations. Tell them that meaningful art is art that speaks to you, that enables you to see life and your faith more clearly. More important than knowing exactly what the artist is trying to say is your response to the art.

Which of these prints on the wall says something to you or addresses your life? What other paintings have done that?

POEM DISCUSSION

The purpose of this discussion is to let the poem "We Are Transmitters" illuminate facts about the lives of the group members and their relationship

77

to Christianity. Your role is that of a good question-asker and a good listener. If you think of better questions than these, keeping in mind the purpose of grounding the poem in the youth's experience, ask them.

Be prepared to phrase each question in alternate ways, in case a youth asks, "Can you say that another way? I'm not sure I understand."

Begin by reading aloud Mark 4:24: ". . . the measure you give will be the measure you get, and still more will be given you."

Pass out a copy of the poem to each person. Ask one youth to read the poem aloud all the way through. (You may want to give him advance notice.)

Then ask someone to read the first two lines aloud and ask: What do you see when you hear the word "transmitter"? What does a transmitter do? What does "transmitting life" mean to you? What other words would you use (creating humanness, giving vitality)? Whom do you know who transmits life? How? Whom do you remember from a movie or book who failed to transmit life and through whom life failed to flow? How? When have you transmitted life? When have you failed to transmit life?

Ask another youth to read the next two lines aloud; then ask: What emotion do you feel when you hear those lines? Embarrassment? Anger? What does the "mystery of sex" symbolize? What does this mean: "Sexless people transmit nothing"?

Ask someone to read the next three lines aloud. What is it like to transmit life into our work?

When have you worked (perhaps on a school project) with enthusiasm and creativity and felt rewarded by more enthusiasm and creative possibilities?

Ask another to read the next five lines aloud. Can we transmit life only if we are artists or professional persons or straight-A students? Into what situations can we put our whole being? Name some other situations with the potential for "life transfusions." Into what situation this week would you like to pour some life?

Ask someone to read the next four lines aloud. Does transmitting life mean giving people whatever they want? Where have you witnessed someone giving what he thought was help to a person who needed something different or needed to discover his own solution? Who are the "living dead"? When do they "eat you up"? (When you let them take advantage of you?) Jesus gave of himself constantly, but when did he refuse to give people what they wanted? (Overturning tables in the temple, Matthew 21:12-13; refusing to be the political hero, Matthew 4:8-10, John 6:15.)

Ask another to read the last two lines aloud. Where did Jesus "kindle the life quality"? Where have you "kindled the life quality"? Do you see an opportunity for "kindling the life quality" this week or in the near future? What is the one thing the author has said to you?

WORSHIP

Close with prayer that the lives of your group may be rekindled in faith.

A FAITH LOOK AT BABBITT

by GEORGE A. LAWSON and RHODA LAWSON BARBER

Major assignment required for this meeting

PREPARATION

Everyone participating should read the novel *Babbitt* by Sinclair Lewis before arriving at the meeting. It is imperative that the leader read the novel. Round up copies from branches of the public library or order paperbacks from a bookstore well in advance of the meeting. Pass out the copies of *Babbitt* at least two weeks before the discussion date and ask the youth to read it "with their theological glasses on." You may wish to pass out a list of questions to stimulate thinking as they read, such as: Where do you see compassion? boredom? hope? hypocrisy? Christian behavior? unchristian behavior?

This meeting should be held in a comfortable room where youth can sit on the floor or sprawl on lounge furniture.

The method of discussion used for this meeting hits several levels. First, let the youth respond with impressions they remember from the book. Then ask more reflective questions. Finally, encourage them to relate the book to their lives theologically by asking in several ways, "What does that have to do with you?" It is important not to confuse the three levels by jumping from one back to another. The discussion will be most effective if you keep the conversation on the topic at hand and discourage rambling. Don't ask too many questions and don't let the length of the discussion exceed the interest span of the youth.

PROCESS

This method of discussion can be used for any art form. It is especially helpful after a group has seen a film together. Below are some sample questions; don't announce the topical names, as these are guidelines for you.

1. IMPRESSIONISTIC QUESTIONS

What exterior (outdoor) scenes do you remember? (Zenith, fishing in Maine) What interior scenes do you recall? (Babbitt's house, office) What sounds do you remember? What minor character sticks out in your mind? What lines of dialogue struck you? What objects do you recall?

Paul Tillich has defined a symbol as anything representative of a deeper reality. What symbols were used in *Babbitt*? (car, cigar, cigar lighter)

2. REFLECTIVE QUESTIONS

Whom did you like? dislike? With whom did you identify? Were you surprised? What was the role of women in the book?
Read:

"They're getting so they don't have a single bit of respect for you. The old-fashioned coon was a fine old cuss—he knew his place—but these young dinges don't want to be porters or cotton-pickers. Oh, no! They got to be lawyers and professors and Lord knows what all! I tell you, it's becoming a pretty serious problem. We ought to get together and show the black man, yes, and the yellow man, his place. Now, I haven't got one particle of race-prejudice. I'm the first to be glad when a nigger succeeds—so long as he stays where he belongs and doesn't try to usurp the rightful authority and business ability of the white man."[1]

Whom do you know who talks like that?
Read:

"What is not generally understood is that this whole industrial matter isn't a question of economics. It's essentially and only a matter of Love, and of the practical application of the Christian religion! Imagine a factory— instead of committees of workmen alienating the boss,

[1] Sinclair Lewis, *Babbitt*, Signet Classic Edition (New York: Harcourt Brace Jovanovich, Inc. 1922, 1950), p. 120. Reprinted by permission of the publisher. © by Sinclair Lewis.

the boss goes among them smiling, and they smile back, the elder brother and the younger. Brothers, that's what they must be, loving brothers, and then strikes would be as inconceivable as hatred in the home!"[2]

This excerpt portrays one image of the church in Babbitt's day. What other images of the church do you recall? (Zillah's Pentecostalism)

What emotions were expressed in the book? Where did you see emotion? What emotions did you experience as you read, and where?

Where were you shocked? What music would you have played for a certain scene? What was your mood at the end of the book?

Where were feelings and opinions expressed honestly? Where were they repressed or distorted? Where did you notice pride or refusal to consider another's opinion? Where did you see inconsistency or hypocrisy? Where did people compromise their beliefs?

Where did you notice a change in a character other than Babbitt? What was Babbitt's goal in life at the beginning of the book?

Read:

Just as he was an Elk, a Booster, and a member of the Chamber of Commerce, just as the priests of the Presbyterian Church determined his every religious belief and the senators who controlled the Republican Party decided in little smoky rooms in Washington what he should think about disarmament, tariff, and Germany, so did the large national advertisers fix the surface of his life, fix what he believed to be his individuality.[3]

What does that show about Babbitt's style? When did Babbitt seem most human to you? When did

he fail? When did you feel the most pity for Babbitt?

Three quotes reveal changes in Babbitt's life:

He was haunted by the ancient thought that somewhere must exist the not impossible she who would understand him, value him, and make him happy.[4]

Thus it came to him merely to run away was folly, because he could never run away from himself.[5]

". . . I've never done a single thing I've wanted to in my whole life! I don't know's I've accomplished anything except just get along. I figure out I've made about a quarter of an inch out of a possible hundred rods. . . . Well, maybe you'll carry things on further, I don't know. But I do get a kind of sneaking pleasure out of the fact that you knew what you wanted to do and did it. . . . Don't be scared of the family. No, nor all of Zenith. Nor of yourself, the way I've been. Go ahead, old man! The world is yours."[6]

In which case did Babbitt see his situation most clearly?

What was Babbitt's problem or struggle? How did he deal with it?

Does Babbitt remind you of anyone you know? Where do you see yourself in Babbitt? That is, where do you see his problems in your life?

Briefly, what is the book about?

3. THEOLOGICAL QUESTIONS

When were Babbitt's illusions destroyed? When did he realize his finiteness and know he couldn't ultimately plan and control his life? We can call this the activity of God.

---

[2] *Ibid.,* pp. 251-252.
[3] *Ibid.,* pp. 80-81.

[4] *Ibid.,* p. 236.
[5] *Ibid.,* p. 242.
[6] *Ibid.,* p. 319.

Paul Tillich speaks of sin as separation from God, self, and others. Where does this separation occur in the book?

Read: "Whatever the misery, he could not regain contentment with a world which, once doubted, became absurd."[7] Have you ever experienced anything similar? When do you think Babbitt was free? When was he not free?

Read:

"Ought to be ashamed, bullying her. Maybe there is her side to things. Maybe she hasn't had such a bloomin' hectic time herself. But I don't care! Good for her to get waked up a little. And I'm going to keep free. Of her and Tanis and the fellows at the club and everybody. I'm going to run my own life!"[8]

How does this compare with Christ's message of love? Can a Christian really run his own life? When did Babbitt live some aspect of Christ's lifestyle? When did he seek to do the right thing, rather than seek the approval of man? (Refused the Good Citizen's League)

How did Christ's rebellion against status quo (Matthew 23) differ from Babbitt's? How else do Christ and Babbitt differ?

Read:

Instantly all the indignations which had been dominating him and the spiritual dramas through which he had struggled became pallid and absurd before the ancient and overwhelming realities, the standard and traditional realities, of sickness and menacing death, the long night, and the thousand steadfast implications of married life. He crept back to her. As she drowsed away in the tropic languor of morphia, he sat on the edge of

[7] *Ibid.,* p. 236.
[8] *Ibid.,* p. 295.

her bed, holding her hand, and for the first time in many weeks her hand abode trustfully in his.[9]

When has an important event made your worries and complaints seem trivial or forced you to reevaluate your situation?

What statements about life does this story suggest?

How is *Babbitt* similar to other stories you have read or seen portrayed on the screen?

4. CLOSING

In conclusion, read the author's note to *The Web and the Rock* by Thomas Wolfe:

This novel is about one man's discovery of life and the world . . . through fantasy and illusion, through falsehood and his own foolishness, through being . . . egotistical and aspiring and hopeful and believing and confused, and pretty much what every one of us is, and goes through . . . and becomes.[10]

Then, read a segment of Joan of Arc's trial from *The Lark* by Jean Anouilh:

CAUCHON: You are saying . . . that the real miracle of God . . . is man. Man, who is naught but sin and error, impotent against his own wickedness—

JOAN: And man is also strength and courage and splendor in his most desperate minutes. I know man because I have seen him. He is a miracle.[11]

Let the quotes sink in silence, without your trying to moralize with them.

[9] *Ibid.,* p. 305.
[10] Thomas Wolfe, *The Web and the Rock* from Charles L. Wallis, ed., *Speaker's Resources from Contemporary Literature* (New York: Harper & Row, Publishers, 1965), page 183.
[11] Jean Anouilh, *The Lark,* translated and adapted by Jean Anouilh (New York: Random House, 1956), page 171.

HOW DO YOU FEEL?

by WAYNE MAJORS

PURPOSE

To understand what emotions are and how to handle them.

INTRODUCTION

Joe—"How do you feel about Sue?"

Bill—"Sue? I think Sue is a . . ."

There is a great difference in what you think and what you feel. You think with your mind, but your feelings are more physical than that. Your emotions often express themselves right in the "pit of your stomach." It's the difference between what goes through your mind and what happens within you when you almost have a head-on collision on the highway. Your mind says, "I'm going to die or be hurt." Your stomach knots up and adrenaline is pumped into your system and you feel *fear*. Fear is the emotion. *I'm going to die* is the thought.

In the two-sentence conversation at the beginning of this lesson, Joe asked for Bill's emotion, and Bill replied with his thought. Bill's best response might have been, "I'm very angry with Sue." That would have been a simple statement of his feeling or emotion.

We find it difficult to speak about emotions. To reveal our emotions is to let another person know what's inside of us, and we usually guard our inner feelings like a secret treasure. Keeping our emotions a secret can be dangerous in several ways. It can keep us at a distance from other people. We never let them know us completely; we only let them know what we think. Also, doctors have known for years that holding emotions inside can make a person physically or mentally ill. If you are angry, for example, and you keep your anger in you, it can give you an upset stomach or even ulcers. A poster slogan that expresses this says, "When I repress my emotions, my stomach keeps score."

In this session, we will try to learn what emotions are and how to handle them in ways that will be harmless to ourselves and others.

PLANS

GETTING STARTED

Ask the question, "What are emotions?" List the responses on chalkboard or newsprint. Try to arrive at a definition that the group can agree with and understand. Perhaps a composite of their responses will be best. It might be helpful at this point to examine the definitions in a dictionary.

Next, make a list of emotions on chalkboard or newsprint with each person in the group helping to make the list. Edit the list, marking out feelings expressed in general terms, such as "good," "bad," "nice," "rotten." Try to make it a list of specific emotions. When the group is satisfied that the list is complete, they may want to share examples of the times when they have felt each of the emotions on the list.

In case the group fails to come up with a list of emotions, here are some to work with: confident, excited, loved, accepted, appreciated, needed, embarrassed, hurt, ambivalent, shocked, aghast, overwhelmed, resentful, angry, furious, hateful, revengeful, guilty, anxious, afraid, annoyed, irritated, rattled, confused, nervous, neglected, shut out, ignored, misunderstood, unappreciated, belittled, and put down.

DISCUSSION

At this point you may want to discuss some or all of the following questions:

- Are some emotions good and some bad?
- Which are good?
- Which are bad?
- What makes us say that one is good and another is bad? (If we do.)

- Would it be better to say that some emotions are "comfortable" and some are "uncomfortable" instead of good and bad? Why or why not?
- Can you fake an emotion?

ROLE PLAY

CHARACTERS

SAM: A newspaper delivery boy who must deliver papers each day or he will lose his route. This job is very important because Sam's family is poor and they need the money. Sam has an old bike that he rides on his paper route. The bike is Sam's most prized possession and almost his only one.

SAM'S FATHER: He works for the city street department and worries constantly about making enough money to take care of his family. Sam's paper route is important to him too; it is the only way Sam can have clothes and books for school.

PETE: Sam's best friend who lives in the house behind Sam.

DIRECTIONS

Write out the description of each of the characters on cards or paper and make name tags for each character. Ask for volunteers to do the role play. Read Part I and role-play it, continuing the role play past the point where the bike is discovered. Then stop and discuss what happened:
- What emotions did Sam feel?
- How did he express them?
- What emotions did his father feel?
- How did he express them?
- How did Sam and his father respond to each other's emotions?

Part I: Sam had a newspaper route, and he had an old bicycle that he rode each morning to deliver his papers. This morning he picked up his papers from his front porch, rolled each one carefully, and

filled his bag. He carried it outside to his bike in the backyard. When he turned the corner of the house, there was his bike—fenders smashed, spokes kicked in, and the basket torn off. Someone had destroyed it during the night. Sam's father comes outside and sees Sam and the bike.

Part II: Pete is eating breakfast when he hears Sam and his father in the next yard. He goes over and sees the bike. He offers Sam his bike to use on the paper route.

After acting out Part II, discuss it, using these questions:
- How did Pete feel when he saw the bike?
- How did he express his emotion?
- How did Sam feel when Pete offered to let him use his bike?
- How did he express it?
- What other ways could Sam, his father, and Pete have expressed their feelings?

LOOKING AT SCRIPTURE

Read the following Scripture passages and discuss:

Matthew 21:10-13 What were Jesus' emotions? How did he express them?

John 12:1-8 What feelings were probably present in this story? Mary's feelings? Jesus' feelings? Judas' feelings? How did they express them?

Matthew 22:37-40 Is Jesus talking about emotions? How do we express these kinds of emotions?

Ask: How can we best express our emotions? Is talking about them enough? Should we act them out? If so, how? If not, why not? What must be taken into consideration when we decide to act out our emotions?

Close with prayer.

83

Section 2
CELEBRATION RESOURCES

Creating Your Own Worship
Worship/Celebration Programs
Songs and Readings for Celebration

PLANNING WORSHIP/CELEBRATION

by ROBERT T. HOWARD

"When I see a stately tree or a delicate flower or a beautiful sunset, I worship," one person told me. He was explaining why he didn't attend the church any longer. "I don't need all that activity or those people to help me worship. It's personal between God and me."

Another expressed it this way: "Everything is too formal and dry in the church's worship. It's like an act everyone is putting on, but nobody really believes it, they've done it so many times. It doesn't touch *today's* needs."

There are others who offer the complaint that modern trends in worship are ruining its meaning. "Bringing guitars and banners into the church, using common language and informal dress is giving up the dignity God deserves," one stated.

"How can it be genuine worship when everything is so carefully planned?" asked still another. "I can't believe God moves according to the instructions of an order of worship prepared by some preacher or committee. Worship ought to be free and open, so real feelings can flow."

Together, these voices raise a valid concern about worship: how can it be *personal, contemporary, traditional,* and *spontaneous* at the same time? Anyone given the task of planning worship is faced with this multiple dilemma. Given the variety of expectation found among most congregations, planning for worship is perhaps more difficult than ever before.

However, there is a way to meet this apparently impossible demand. Worship planners do not have to give in to the loudest voices or those with the strongest urges. In fact, a responsible committee can often help a congregation or a youth group widen its experience through a serious attempt to make worship personal, contemporary, traditional, and spontaneous.

No worship format or single worship service will meet the varied needs in a congregation. Where there is freedom for change in worship patterns, the needs of more persons will be met.

THE COMMITTEE'S TASK

The committee responsible for planning worship should first carefully recognize its purpose. Planning worship is not a matter of deciding what will be done and said, by whom and when, in order *to make worship happen.* Genuine worship cannot be forced or required; it must be released by those who worship. The task of the planning committee, then, is to determine what actions, moods, and music, in what sequence, will help release the experience of worship for persons in the congregation.

Essential to this task is the admission that the planning doesn't make worship occur. The work of the committee still leaves room for the unexpected, the spontaneous, the personal event to appear in worship. There may be "open" places in the format—for instance, a brief period of silence or a call for personal response to a reading —or simply an implied openness to hymns and other congregational actions. The worshipers, not the plan, make the experience.

This approach obviously requires a keen sensitivity by the committee members. In their planning, they must be aware of the basic concerns and experiences of the people who form the congregation. Some helpful survey questions at this point are: "What events (victories, losses) have affected some of these people recently?" "What happenings do several people hold in common as part of their relationship?" "How will these events and happenings be included in the worship potential?" The committee's main purpose is to provide a setting in which the lives of the people may be opened, touched, and reaffirmed by the claims of the gospel of God.

COMMUNITY IN CELEBRATION

Another key to the committee's work is an understanding of the purpose of worship. The primary reason a group assembles for worship is to achieve some goal of the whole group; it is a community experience. While on a given day the group's need may be the sharing of grief at the death of some beloved member, the continuing objective of worship is preparation for being the "salt of the earth," active participants in God's continuing creation of the world.

This preparation includes accepting the past week's events—their losses as well as victories—and finding strength from them. It includes reaffirming each person's belonging in the community of faith. It includes renewal of concern for and commitment to the work of the gospel in the world. In summary, in worship people are celebrating the fact that "God is at work among us."

The committee, then, sees the worship experience as an opportunity to strengthen the life of the community of faith, and encourage the lives of individual members for their service in the world. The ideal worship experience will conclude with the people eager to "go back to work" with a renewal of commitment to affect the world with the gospel.

GUIDELINES FOR PLANNING WORSHIP

Here are some general helps for a committee to follow in determining the most likely "openings" through which expression of life and faith can be made by a specific congregation.

HARMONY OF MOOD

Regardless of other interests carried by participants in worship, the experience must give high priority to a conscious recognition of God's role in the "dialogue." To include this concern in the planning, there are several moods which need to be allowed in the worship. These moods emerge from the meaning of the Christian faith. Whatever they may be called, they include such expressions as praise, thanksgiving, confession, forgiveness, intercession, inspiration, dedication, response, and commitment.

Whether in various combinations or in a different order, these moods should be part of the worship experience. Through such openings the central features of the faith are given opportunity to touch lives. It is also through the inclusion of these moods that the genuine traditions of earlier generations are maintained, thus not only strengthening a dependence on God, but keeping worship in a historical perspective.

Important to this guideline is the achievement of harmony in these moods. Overdrawn or inappropriate emphasis at any point can weaken the depth of worship. The shifting from one mood to another should be clear but not too abrupt. They should build toward a peak at the conclusion of worship, usually ending with response or dedication.

Conscious expression of these moods is essential to the celebration of a faithful people.

BALANCE OF TONE

Another guideline for planning worship recognizes the keen balance needed in congregational participation. Each person brings attitudes, feelings, experiences, needs, hopes, and expectations when he arrives for worship. Opportunities for expressing these should be made a part of the worship. At the same time, members of the congregation need to reaffirm the shared experience of the community.

The committee can seek to give each of these tones a means of expression. By various actions and elements of involvement, the worshiping community can see itself accepting the "offerings" of its members for joint celebration and thus give recognition both to the personal and corporate significance of worship.

Achievement of balance between these two tones depends upon knowledge of the congregation. Not only is the readiness of the congregation for sharing its community life important, but the elements of expression acceptable to the worshipers must be evaluated and used wisely.

FLOW OF ENERGY

The planning committee should also give concern to the "life" of worship. Unless there is authentic involvement and enthusiasm, worship is cold. There also must be a pattern to the flow of energy to prevent an incomplete experience.

For instance, the attention of the worshipers on personal needs is valid, but should not receive the heaviest emphasis of energy. An opportunity for the community to hear and respond to the revelation of God is also necessary to the celebration. This subjective-objective flow is another key to help the committee.

To design a worship format which encourages energetic involvement is important. Helping worshipers to become responsible for the achievement of worship is not an easy task but is necessary to insure a complete experience. This includes an active "listening" by the congregation and permits the faith dialogue necessary to Christian worship.

PUTTING IT TOGETHER

Using these guidelines, the planning committee may select elements which help achieve their potential. There is a wide variety of resources available.

Hymns, prayers, responsive readings, litanies, anthems, special music, Scripture readings, unison statements, the sermon, the offering, and other more common elements become instruments in the enabling of worship.

One of the secondary responsibilities of the planning committee is to become familiar with newer actions to include in worship. These should be introduced to the congregation whenever there are opportunities, because worship should always be contemporary, not just on those occasions when a special format is followed. Thoughtful preparation and sensitive concern for the growing edge of the congregation can make such discovery a continuing experience.

Resources available to the committee may be found in several service books. Many more recently published books offer suggestions about newer elements, including use of multimedia. Some books which a committee will find helpful are:

Multi-Media Worship: A Model and Nine Viewpoints, Myron B. Bloy, Jr., ed. New York: The Seabury Press, Inc., 1969.

Ways of Worship for New Forms of Mission, Scott Francis Brenner. New York: Friendship Press, 1968.

Contemporary Worship Services, James L. Christensen. Old Tappan, New Jersey: Fleming H. Revell Company, 1971.

There is no single "secret" to effective celebration. Planning helps to eliminate unnecessary barriers and encourage the free expression of life—both the life of the community and the life God will provide—through Christian worship.

CELEBRATING OUR TOGETHERNESS
by GEORGE A. LAWSON

PURPOSE

This worship experience should emphasize the intentional, decisional, serving nature of Christianity and encourage a sense of group corporateness rather than individualism.

CONTEXT

This service could be used to conclude a retreat or celebrate a completed project or graduation.

THE ROOM

The room should contain various elements which will suggest the theme. Art prints (in various styles) of the Lord's Supper and those expressing the brokenness of life (e.g., Picasso's *Guernica*) and the unity of life (e.g., Picasso's *Mother and Child*) may be used.

On a poster, place this quote from Eugene O'Neill's *The Great God Brown*:[1] "BROWN: Man is born broken. He lives by mending. The grace of God is glue!"

Use a rectangular table or a number of tables arranged in a square or rectangle. In the center (on an additional small table if you follow the latter plan) arrange some objects that will draw attention to the worship theme (Christian symbols, broken objects, a chalice, sculpture, a candle). Place a loaf of French bread at the leader's place and a small cup of juice at each place. If some of the "broken things" were broken because of some event in the life of the group, they could have a special meaning and significance.

THE SERVICE

The leader may be a youth, an advisor, or the minister. He or she leads the group in singing a few songs. Suggestions: (1) hymn "For All the Saints," stopping between verses to call out names of great humanitarians and churchmen, e.g., Martin Luther King, Jr., Albert Schweitzer, or a member of the group; (2) Psalm 117 (as it appears in the *Songbook of the Ecumenical Institute,* Chicago); (3) words the group has composed to sing

---

[1] Eugene O'Neill, *The Great God Brown* from Charles L. Wallis, ed., *Speaker's Resources from Contemporary Literature,* (New York: Harper & Row, Publishers, 1965), p. 115. Used with permission of Random House, Inc.

to popular tunes like "Amazing Grace." Encourage free body movement such as foot stomping, hand clapping, swaying, and tapping on chairs and tables to begin the worship with an enthusiastic, celebrative quality.

When everyone is seated, the leader asks: "What does it mean to worship God in the midst of the twentieth century's scientific and cultural revolutions? Worship should include full participation by everyone; it should be a rehearsal of the way life is; it should enable us to be totally obedient to God and live a life of involvement, of giving ourselves to others."

A youth leads the group in an antiphonal psalm reading.

The leader then leads a five-minute conversation asking the group to respond to these questions: What are some objects used in the Communion service? When has Communion been meaningful for you? What does Communion symbolize for you today as a modern Christian?

A youth reads 1 Corinthians 11:23b-26.

The leader breaks the loaf and points out that a meaning of the Communion bread is that it represents the brokenness of life. (Life never seems to turn out the way we expect it to.) He pours juice into his glass from a container and says that it symbolizes the "spilled-outness" of life, our capacity to give of ourselves in the midst of the brokenness.

The leader passes the loaf around the table. Each person breaks off a piece, eats it, and drinks the juice. The leader announces that sentence prayers for church and world problems may be offered. (They are begun by a couple of youth who have been asked in advance.) As each person concludes his sentence with "Amen," the group responds with "Amen" or the chorus of the spiritual "Amen," thus affirming that the prayer is not only that of an individual but of the group.

The group sings a concluding song, such as "They'll Know We Are Christians by Our Love."

Group Benediction: Go forth into the world in peace; be of good courage; hold fast to that which is good; render to no man evil for evil; strengthen the faint-hearted; support the weak; help the afflicted; honor all men; love and serve the Lord, rejoicing in the power of the Holy Spirit. Amen.

91

MEANING IN A FIRE

by JERRY L. BELDEN

MATERIALS NEEDED

Supplies Needed

1. A well-built campfire that will burn approximately two hours
2. Cassette tape player
3. Cassette tape of selected Christian folk music
4. Books—*God Is Beautiful, Man* and *God Is for Real, Man,* both by Carl F. Burke (Association Press, New York)

SETTING

Out of doors around campfire or indoors around fireplace. Only light is that of the fire.

PERSONS NEEDED TO LEAD SERVICE

One person can lead the worship service, but the service will have much more meaning if more than one person leads it. For example, one person with a guitar could lead the singing; another person could read the Scripture; and another person lead the group conversation.

THE SERVICE

TAPED MUSIC

Christian folk music

GROUP SINGING

Sing songs informally. Use songs which the group knows. Some suggestions are: "He's Got the Whole World in His Hands," "Jacob's Ladder," "Let Us Break Bread Together," "Lord, I Want to Be a Christian."

SCRIPTURE

1. "When a Man Gets Pulled Out" (John 3:1-21) from *God Is for Real, Man* by Carl F. Burke.
2. "Getting Sins Fixed Up" (Acts 10:34) from *God Is Beautiful, Man* by Carl F. Burke.

GROUP SINGING

Sing some more songs informally or have someone sing a solo, perhaps with guitar accompaniment.

GROUP CONVERSATION

Using tongs or two long sticks, remove several coals of varying sizes from the fire, each coal being left several inches apart from any other coal. Allow the group to watch the separated coals for three or four minutes, noticing that the glow of the coals by themselves gets dimmer by the moment. Then put the coals into the fire to burn once again.

Encourage the group members to talk about their thoughts as they watch the coals losing their glow.

Then ask: If we are Christians, can we be on fire? How? How can we keep our fire going and our life aglow?

CLOSING

Ask the members of the worshiping congregation to join hands in friendship in a circle. Then tell them that following a closing prayer, each person should affirm the other members of the worshiping congregation with a handshake, a "God bless you," an embrace, or some other meaningful expression. Pray a simple, meaningful, brief prayer, expressing what has happened in the worship service.

92

Use of cameras, records, art, live music, and the spoken word to create worship in a new format

REJOICE IN THE LORD: A CELEBRATION
by PATSY C. PETERSON

INTRODUCTION

Describing in words a worship/celebration like the one suggested in these pages is very difficult. The full dimension of meaningfulness can be captured only through active participation in the service. The reader should keep in mind that the accurate "translation" results when the ideas set forth here are adapted and used in his or her own local setting.

This celebration is based upon the words of Psalm 118:24 and Philippians 4:4. The most authentic worship/celebration events come through a group process of shared experience. We have many gifted youth in our midst today, and this service is designed for a group of youth to dedicate their time and talents to God and praise him in a service of joyfulness.

The following pattern of suggestions is only a guide for directing youth to express, on a high, affirmative note through visual images, music, and spoken word that Christians truly have something to CELEBRATE. The pattern set forth in these pages is of a multimedia nature, since there are so many ways in which youth of today can utilize their God-given talents in proclaiming their faith through the various forms of media.

MEDIA

The media suggested for use are:

CAMERAS

Whether simple Instamatic or sophisticated 35mm or super-8mm (movie), cameras are accessible to and used by many youth. Also, the projectors necessary for showing slides and movies are now owned by these same youth or their parents. Photography can be a welcome means for the less verbally oriented person to make significant theological statements.

RECORDS AND TAPE RECORDINGS

These provide another means of meaningful expression of faith. Some contemporary records are especially good for church use. Youth can also make their own tapes of music, sound collages, etc., in creating a worship event.

ART

This has been somewhat neglected in the recent past by the church. Artistically gifted youth can contribute to celebration and church art through designing and making banners. Two simple designs for banners which could be utilized in this celebration are shown at the beginning of this chapter.

LIVE MUSIC

This has had a long and important role in communicating the faith. In addition to vocal music, guitar, trumpet, and organ are suggested for use in the service outlined in these pages. These instruments mentioned are intended to serve only as indicators of how various musical instruments can be an integral part of celebration. Instrumentalists are a great enhancement to a celebrative event.

WORDS

The verbal aspect is not to be neglected, as it is a vital means of communication. Encourage youth gifted in writing to prepare poetic and prose materials to be used at appropriate points of the service.

OUTLINE

A basic outline for "Rejoice in the Lord":
BECOME
Preparing

Greeting
Questioning
Replying
Affirming
REJOICE
Proclaiming through song
Proclaiming words and visual images
Affirming through song
BEGIN
Challenging
Dedicating and giving
Taking form

THE EVENT

A good starting point for implementing this outline is to select a core group of youth and one or two adult facilitators who will be responsible for preparing the worship event. With the aid of the more detailed information below, this core group can develop an event for its own local setting and needs.

BECOME

As participants begin to gather for the celebration, they can be given some orientation for the overall mood of the event by having recorded music playing before the first formal greeting. Some selections that can be used for this are: selections from the album *Switched-On Bach* (Columbia); "Classical Gas" from the album *Mason Williams Phonograph Record* (Warner Brothers-Seven Arts); "Joy" (Mega—45 r.p.m.); and "Popcorn" (Musicor—45 r.p.m.).

The initial moments of the celebration are important for the development of a spirit of community. A brief, informal, responsive call to worship is an excellent first step. Youth gifted in verbalizing can contribute at this point. The greeting should incorporate Scripture passages mentioned in the Introduction.

With the mention of rejoicing and gladness in the greeting, a rather natural question might arise with respect to how it can be possible to rejoice and be glad. A predetermined person can raise this question. Here again, a verbally gifted person could prepare a "script." Headlines could be used

in a creative manner to suggest the context of life and worship.

The reply to the question can then move into the audio-visual element of the celebration. The use of the recording "Lean on Me" by Bill Withers (Sussex—45 r.p.m.) and accompanying slides which complement visually the words of the song can be effective. A challenging presentation results if slides are projected with two projectors. One projector could contain slides depicting struggles of mankind. This projector should be started at the same time as the record. The second projector could contain slides of Christ symbols, i.e., pictures of Christ, crosses, and other Christian symbols. (The pictures of Christ can be obtained by taking a photograph of large pictures found in most churches.) The other slides could be handmade by methods described in "How to Make Slides" in *Respond, Volume 2.* The second projector should not be started until the line of the song lyric, "Lean on me when you're not strong." The first projector should be turned off with the conclusion of the music, but the second projector showing Christian symbols should continue to flash slides on the screen for several seconds during a period of silence following the end of the record. Thus the emphasis is placed upon the importance of a Christ-centered life.

A time of corporate sharing following the record and slides can be developed through spontaneous responses to the statement: "To be a Christian is like. . . ." This method of sharing will further facilitate the community aspect of worship. (One person might give a brief explanation of how simile is used as a creative litany. Through this method each person is provided opportunity to make his own affirmation of faith. Some may choose to remain silent, and it must be understood that for some silence is a more meaningful participation than open participation.)

REJOICE

When the affirmations of faith have been made, the stage is set for active rejoicing. Philippians 4:4 set to music in round form can be the invitation to rejoice.

Observe Repeat Signs

Re - joice in the Lord al - ways, and a -

gain I say re - joice. Re - joice! Re -

joice, and a - gain I say re-joice.

When first group starts second line, the second
group starts first line; when second group starts
second line, the third group starts first line; etc.;
etc.

Banners can be brought into the place of worship and put in appropriate positions as the congregation is singing the round.

Additional songs which can be used to follow the singing of the round and the placing of the banners are: "All You Peoples, Clap Your Hands" by Ray Repp, "Clap Your Hands" by Paul Quinlan, and "To Be Alive" by Ray Repp from *Hymnal for Young Christians, Volume 2* (Chicago: F.E.L. Publications, Ltd., 1969); verses 1 and 2 of "This Is the Day" by Cyril A. Reilly and Roger Nachtwey from *Hymns for Now II* (St. Louis: Concordia Publishing House, 1969). Guitar accompaniment is especially good for all of the above songs. In addition to the hymnals mentioned previously, *Songbook for Saints and Sinners* by Carlton R. Young (Carol Stream, Ill.: agápe, 1971) is a good collection of hymns of contemporary nature and is helpful when a search is being made for songs for contemporary celebration.

For a change of pace, further proclamation can be made with the use of a super-8mm movie planned and prepared by youth. The film should show local scenes depicting: (1) life struggles, (2) life in Christ, (3) life as Christian celebration. The sound track of the movie can be composed of readings of creative writing of young people or taped music or a sound collage reflecting the moods of the visual images appearing on the screen.

Affirmation of the celebrative ending of the movie can be the community singing of the carol "Joy to the World." Singing this carol at times other than the Christmas season can be very significant.

96

BEGIN

Celebration truly begins when one accepts the challenge for Christian involvement in the humdrum of the everydayness in the world. Typical everyday-type needs and situations can be reviewed and a challenge made to meet these in the strength of Christ. This segment of the event provides another opportunity for the spoken word prepared for the community by those gifted with verbalizing.

At the conclusion of the challenge, each person can be requested to write on a slip of paper one specific time during the coming week that he will dedicate to assist someone with a specific, known need. These offerings can be brought forward to a designated place. If physical surroundings permit, a rustic cross can be in view at all times during the service, and the offerings can be placed at the base of the cross. As people move forward and then return to their places, "Joyful, Joyful We Adore Thee" can be played by organ and trumpet. A trumpet descant makes for a more interesting offertory. One descant that can be used is:

Trumpet in D   by David Barger

A time of silence is recommended following the offering. Then one of the worship leaders can quote the words to "Christ Takes Form" by Kent Schneider. (The words and music to "Christ Takes Form" can be obtained by writing to The Center for Contemporary Celebration, 1400 East 53rd Street, Chicago, IL 60615.) The leader can then invite the community to participate in singing this benediction. An effective way to do this is to have the community sing the hymn two or three times and then, continuing to sing, move into the world.

NOTE

This worship/celebration entails planning and participation on the part of many people. The most rewarding facet of a service like this is that encounter with God becomes reality as individuals come together in shared experiences of "being in Christ."

REJOICE IN THE LORD!
AND
AGAIN I SAY REJOICE!

WE ARE THE CHURCH
by JERRY L. BELDEN

MATERIALS NEEDED

1. Number of chairs, placed in a circle, equaling the number of persons present
2. Record player
3. Recording of *Jesus Christ Superstar*
4. Book: Carl F. Burke, *Treat Me Cool, Lord* (New York: Association Press, 1968)
5. Songbook, *Hymns for Now* (Concordia Publishing House)
6. Paper cups, one for every four members of the worshiping congregation
7. *New English Bible*

SETTING

The place of worship can be anywhere the worshiping congregation can come together in a flexible circle, sitting on the floor or on chairs.

LEADERSHIP

One person can lead this worship experience, but if more than one person leads, it will be more meaningful. For example, if one person leads in the call to worship, the prayer, and the benediction, another person with a guitar could lead the singing, and a third person could then lead the action experience.

ORDER OF SERVICE

MUSIC

Play selections from *Jesus Christ Superstar*.

CALL TO WORSHIP

"Let each of us share what we believe the world needs most, in one word, as our call to worship."

The members of the worshiping congregation will then respond by saying many things like "Love," "Peace," or "Jesus."

PRAYER

"Everybody's Got the Same Father," pages 84 and 85 of *Treat Me Cool, Lord* by Carl F. Burke.

SONG

"They'll Know We Are Christians"

EXPERIENCE

1. Divide the worshiping congregation into groups of fours (quads).

98

2. Give a paper cup to each quad.

3. The person given the cup is to hold it until the following instructions are given; then that person will begin the action.

- The cup is the church. First person is to do to the cup what he would like to do to the church, nonverbally.

- Then the second person receives the cup (the church) in whatever shape the first person leaves it. He then does to the church (the cup) what he feels needs to be done under the circumstances, without saying a word. After the second person finishes, he passes it on to number three who does what he thinks needs to be done and passes it to number four. Number four then continues to do what he feels needs to be done to the church under the circumstances that he finds it and passes it back to number one.

- Then the quads pass the cup around again, with each person telling what he did to the cup and why.

- After the quads are finished, the number one person will share what happened in his quad with the total worshiping congregation.

4. The leader should then summarize the experience, bringing out the importance of the church in our lives, even though for all of us the church is not perfect and there are many things we would like to change about it.

SCRIPTURE

1 Corinthians 12:12-27 (NEB).

SONG

"Sons of God," page 23 of *Hymns for Now*

BENEDICTION

In closing, the leader asks each one in the group to share how "we are the church" by putting his thoughts into one sentence. In response to this, the leader leads the group in singing a chorus of "Amen," page 11 of *Hymns for Now*.

MUSIC

Selected portions of *Jesus Christ Superstar*

A SUMMONS TO CELEBRATION!

by ROBERT A. NOBLETT

FOR OPENERS

Do you ever get the feeling that we live in an era of gloominess? No question about it, there are many realities that make us feel their crippling tragedy (and indeed as Christians we ought to feel tragedy and do something about it); but we are something less than effective if we bring to such situations only more gloom! Let us suppose that we go out of our home on a cold winter day only to find our car's battery stone dead. So we call the garage for help. But what happens if we find that the battery in the tow truck is just as dead? If we are going to be of significant assistance to other people, we will want to approach with our batteries in tip-top shape and fully energized. Let us think about worship as a reenergizing process and suggest some steps in planning a worship experience around the theme of celebration.

WHAT WE'RE ABOUT

The invitation to worship is not unlike the invitation that is extended to us by any body of water as we stand on its shores. It conveys a certain magnetism and draws us near. We wade in, become familiar with it, and soon find ourselves enjoying it to the hilt. We feel supported and buoyant as we rest on its surface and we feel warm and relaxed as the sun shines down in its fullness. To extend our analogy further, when we come to worship we are attracted by its message of hope, and trust that during our experience of it we are rendered buoyant by our fellow worshipers. Together we break open once again the good news of the gospel and take the nourishment it offers us.

SOME STRUCTURE

THE SUMMONS

Worship is an intentional act which has a beginning and an ending. It opens with a statement of affirmation. Since our theme is to be celebration, have a participant draft a summons to worship which incorporates a sense of gladness and hope. For example:

> Serve the Lord with gladness!
>   Come into his presence with singing! . . .
> Enter his gates with thanksgiving,
>   and his courts with praise!
>   Give thanks to him, bless his name!
> For the Lord is good;
>   his steadfast love endures for ever,
>   and his faithfulness to all generations (Psalm 100:2-5).

That's a traditional one. It would doubtless be more meaningful if a person could write a summons that comes out of personal experience. Something like this may be more authentic and meaningful: "The pace of our lives is often so great that we feel like we are on a merry-go-round that not only goes round and round but up and down as well. I invite you, therefore, to participate in an act of worship through which we will hear once more the good news that God holds us in deepest affection and wants for each of his children happiness and wholeness."

The summons could be delivered by the reading of poetry, or the viewing of a poster, or the playing of music. In ancient Israel, the day of worship began with the blast of a trumpet!

DEVELOPING THE THEME

The theme can be simply declared: "It is our purpose to talk together about celebration." Have the participants list and then share together those things which make them happy and celebrative. Background music played while they are writing could be encouraging. Select music which draws out the theme, such as "My Favorite Things" from *The Sound of Music* or the song "Joy Is Like the Rain" from the album of the same name (Avant Garde, stereo AVS-101).

100

Another method would be to contact the participants some time before the day the worship is to be experienced and have them bring in various media which would express sources of joy—pictures, slides, home movies, cassette recordings, art prints, etc. In either case (you may want to do both), allow for a time of individual elaboration and explanation.

CREATING A COMPOSITE

Concordance Needed

Another vital element in worship is the proclamation of the Word. This portion is usually referred to as the homily or sermon, and its purpose is to bring the wishes of God—as we understand them from biblical faith and present personal experience—to bear on the lives of the worshipers.

We know today, moreover, that there is a great deal of power in a group of people—an infinite amount of understanding, of insight, of energy—and so why not use it in the development of a corporate sermon—a composite of the thoughts and feelings of the group regarding the nature of celebration?

Your church library or your pastor has a biblical concordance, so secure it and find the list of biblical references under the heading "joy." Divide them up among the participants and have them feed back to the group what the various references seem to be suggesting about the essence of joy.

Jot these thoughts down on newsprint. Then have the group think together about what stands behind, what allows for, those happy moments they have spoken of earlier. For example, one person may have written down a family picnic as something which affords deep delight. Why is that? Could it have something to do with the fact that the family cares for each other, listens to each other, supports each other?

Through this process, the worshipers should be able to create a composite sermon on joy or celebration. It would be helpful to summarize and list on newsprint the conclusions. The result might be something like this: Christians celebrate because God loves them; this love has been most deeply expressed in the event of Jesus Christ; and whenever Christians behaviorally reflect the wish of God that his children live together in peace and mutual respect and understanding, they are providing for that moment when happiness and celebration will be decidedly felt.

WRAPPING THINGS UP

Worship calls forth resolve. When we leave the experience, we ought to be different from when we began. Worship is an act of reaffirmation. There should be some sort of commitment made on the part of the participants to give daily embodiment to feelings of celebration and joy. This might be expressed by having the group join hands and sing a favorite hymn or song ("Joyful, Joyful, We Adore Thee" or a popular song which tells of happiness) or engage in unison prayer or simply repeat together the summary of thoughts developed in the composite. At the conclusion of worship, the participants should feel they are in closer touch with themselves, their friends, and God. When this happens, we know worship to be authentic.

JOY!

Suzi Grizzard

© Suzi Grizzard, used by permission.

NEW REALITY

Donald Nelson

Donald Nelson

(Based on the story of the paralytic at the temple gate)

( ) Chords in parentheses are for low voice or for use with capo.

2. And then they came and glanced my way.
   Peter and John their names they say.
   Not a cent have we to give,
   But we can help to make you live.

3. And then they took my trembling hand.
   They lifted me and made me stand.
   Imagine me a-walkin' 'round,
   My happy tears washed the ground.

4. O praise to God for what he's done.
   I'm free again—my battle won.
   Lord, take my hand and guide my way,
   Help me to live my faith each day.

FREEDOM

Debbie New

Bill England

High in the sky the ea-gle soars.   My
spir-it breaks loose and yearns to go with him. To-
geth-er we drive—down, down, down.   Sud-den-ly he
wheels and climbs,   Leav-ing my   spir-it   to
plum-met to the earth be-low,   As the ea-gle
soars in the free-dom of the heav'ns a-bove.

HOW TO LOVE GOD

Connie Ketter

A JOINING OF VOICES

by Richard Orr

(Shouts and exclamations to be used at the beginning of a joyful moment)

We're alive.

Thank you, Lord. Your hand has touched
our dust.
You gave us breathing air and
breathing space.
We thank you, Lord, for the sight and sense
to see the flowers,
to hear the wind,
to feel the waters in our hand,
to sleep with the night and wake with the sun,
to sing praises to you,
to hear your voice in our happenings.
Our hearts are stirred with each new sight and
sound. Like a stream, the whole world pours into
our eyes,
our hands,
and fills our souls with living gladness.
O Lord, our God, continue to surprise us with
joy!

A-A-A men!

HANDLES FOR LEADERS—YOUTH AND ADULTS

GUIDELINES FOR RAISING MONEY
by ROGER W. PRICE

A project to raise money inevitably involves time, effort, and sometimes a preliminary expense. When is a work project a good expenditure of your and your youth group's energy and when is it not? This question sooner or later must be faced.

Very few groups have to earn money to pay for basic youth ministry resources. The great majority of churches consider it their responsibility to provide church school materials and supplies as well as other resources, such as the *Respond* books.

If money must be raised for basic program expense, a lot of time that should be spent in study, fellowship, and worship will be lost. Churches should consider basic resource materials as necessary, such as pews, hymnals, lights, water, and other such items.

Most groups, however, have to seek financial support for special projects, e.g., mission trips, work projects, retreats, camps, special conferences, or for contributing to a special cause.

More and more churches are taking the responsibility of caring for all of the advisors' expenses, especially so on special trips, conferences, or projects. Most adult workers with youth spend a considerable amount of money as it is, on snacks when youth come over, babysitting while they are with the youth group, books, etc. Plan ahead and you may be able to get a special item included in the church budget if a trip or conference is especially expensive to the adults who work with youth.

SHOULD YOU GO THE PROJECT ROUTE?

Many factors need to be considered in evaluating the benefits to be received from a project against the expenditure of time and energy that will be needed. The board of finance or the board of trustees in many churches has rules that regulate the timing and kind of money-raising projects that can be carried out by church groups. You should check your situation to find out whether there are such rules before planning your project.

While there is no clear, objective way to measure the worthwhileness of a project, there are some general guidelines that need to be considered and questions that should be asked.

1. When can planning be accomplished, and can the youth carry out much of the responsibility? Use as little time as possible from your regular activities so that the project doesn't become all-consuming.

2. Are you sure it's worth the effort? It's always possible that work projects are a way of avoiding serious struggles in theology, the Christian life, group cooperation, or another important area of a group's life. Consider those who will benefit and how they will be aided. The comparison between time and effort and probable return must be considered. Some projects take a lot of preparation and work with relatively little financial return.

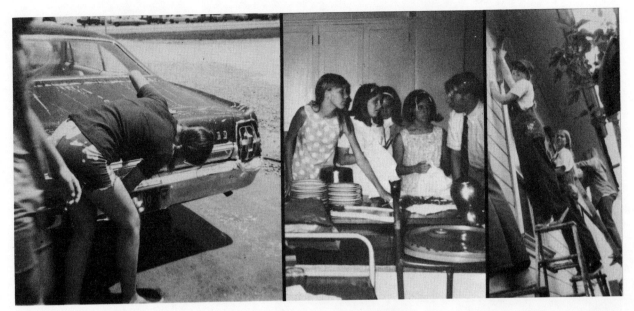

3. Will this particular project be disruptive of time in study, worship, or other areas of group life? Not everyone responds to everything in the same way. Be sure that a young person is not excluded because he can't work on a project or go on a trip.

4. Can you do what you say you will in a project, and can you do it well? It's better to have a smaller project and do it well than fail or do a sloppy job in a larger undertaking. Remember you may want to do another project in the future and that success or failure may be judged on how well you do now.

5. Have enough safety precautions been taken? While something can go wrong anytime and someone may be injured, there are some work projects which by their very nature have more risk of injury than another activity. Who is responsible for medical bills if someone should be injured? Some groups have blanket accident insurance, or insurance may be purchased at a low cost for each activity. Check with an insurance representative in your church to discover if your group is covered or can be covered by a policy.

6. Do you need any special equipment or special skills? If you are going to have a car wash, you need hoses, vacuum cleaners, etc. You also need to decide, for instance, who is going to drive the cars through a car wash, if this is

necessary. Other projects call for their own special equipment.

7. Look ahead to potential problems. Think of various alternatives to problem situations, e.g., rain might affect your project. Include information on the alternate plans in your publicity.

CHOOSING A PROJECT

The number and kind of youth projects to raise money is almost endless. The following activities have all been used in the past with people either paying a set price or making a donation for the service given:

- garage or rummage sale
- bake sale
- car wash
- ice cream social
- Sunday morning breakfast for the whole church
- dramatic play or talent night
- fine arts festival
- hobby show
- chili supper
- sending out mailings (for businesses or other organizations at particular times in the year)
- slave day (Youth are auctioned off for a day to the highest bidder. This event can have the side benefit of providing good youth-adult dialogue.)
- collect bottles, cans, newspapers, etc.
- sell various items, e.g., Christmas cards, candles, candy, etc.
- spook house at Halloween

- dinner at church annual meeting or other special occasion
- decorate a float for a parade, e.g., the Tournament of Roses Parade on New Year's Day in Pasadena, Calif.

Look around. You will find some particular need or interest in your community or church that your group could fulfill.

GETTING THE WORD AROUND

A good job on publicity is desirable for several different reasons. The church needs to know what the youth groups are doing. Many adults who are not in contact with kids seem to develop negative attitudes toward youth from much of what they see and hear in the newspapers and on TV. If you are doing something good, let others know about it. We need more good news.

The congregation will certainly be more willing to support a group's work projects when they know that the receipts are going for a good cause. Publicity may also bring specific donations from some very unexpected sources. Individuals you never thought of before may make a generous contribution because a project is of particular interest to them or they like what the group is doing.

At times, after careful consideration, you might choose to approach a particular individual and ask him or her to make a contribution. Individuals are often most willing to make a special contribution, particularly if it can be arranged so that the

money goes to pay the way of someone who otherwise might not be able to share in a particular event. Some care should be taken so that a young person who has financial problems, whose way is paid, is not embarrassed by having others know about this arrangement. The more privately this can be arranged, the better.

If you do choose to approach individuals or groups (e.g., adult church school classes) to make a contribution to your project, be sure you don't overwork a good thing.

ADVANTAGES OF PROJECTS

Two possible advantages to projects have not yet been mentioned. Work projects have a way of increasing a sense of fellowship in a group as the youth work together on a common task. This factor can often be of great importance.

A work project may also give the adult youth worker an opportunity to work alongside, and informally talk with, a young person who may be quite shy and seemingly unresponsive in a regular group meeting. At times it seems easier to talk while working together on a task than just individual to individual.

Work projects are neither bad or good in and of themselves. How they are used and the way they are carried out determine their value. They can be a very useful tool in accomplishing a particular goal.

111

GUIDELINES FOR SERVICE PROJECTS
by DUANE L. SISSON

THE PLACE TO START

Someone in the youth group feels the group should become involved in a meaningful service project. Now how do you go about it?

At the outset the whole group should get on board. Something like this usually starts with one or two individuals, but the commitment of the group is important if it is to be successful. The group needs to respond in its own way. Groups are like persons. They each have their own personality and interests, their own individual characteristics. What works one place will not work in another. What is true for one group often is not true for another.

The first answer to the question of how the group is to get involved is to discover who you are as a group. Is there real interest in Christian service? Is a service project the task that has top priority for your group at this time or are there other things that must be completed and put together before the group is spiritually ready and mature enough to undertake service for others beyond itself? What kinds of skills do you have to offer? What service is needed in your community? What blocks of time are involved in a specific opportunity for service? Are the members of the group available at the time needed? How about the problems related to regular transportation?

Manufacturing service projects is probably the one thing we should never do. Service is a two-way street. The very fact you feel that your group needs to do something indicates that service is for the group as well as others. We "do" to meet our need as well as the needs of others.

If service is to meet the need of your group, then the leader's responsibility is to help the group define its need for itself. Listening is very important in accomplishing this task. In group life, concerns are voiced in many ways. We need to be aware of what is being said and aid the group in listening to each other. Rather than dumping on the group the idea that they need to do a project, we can support that voice within the group calling for service.

CHOOSING A PROJECT

When a group wants to give to itself, then its members are ready, as a group, to choose a service project. Certainly a criterion for choosing a project is that it must meet a real need. Nothing kills service more than doing something that was manufactured to meet our need and not really to accomplish a task for someone else. A group needs to

112

subordinate its own desire to the goal of fulfilling the needs of the other. This method is not always convenient, but service, real service, as in the good Samaritan story, is seldom convenient.

The group must have an understanding of what it can do, including the time it can give a project. Another thing that can successfully kill the spirit of service is the inability to finish a project.

It is good at the outset to set a time limit on the group's service commitment. Example: "We will agree to provide eight tutors for one-to-one teaching at the community center each Tuesday afternoon from 4:00-6:00 P.M. for eight weeks starting the first of the month." This kind of contract can be completed by the group. If a group starts a task with no ending point in mind, the time of ending is likely to be frustrating and divisive to the group. If the time period in the original contract is fulfilled and the group continues to be enthusiastic, the time can be extended, but a new agreed-upon ending date needs to be clearly established. If there is no sense of completion, even in an ongoing project, a group can develop a real sense of frustration and failure. "We did it!" is not just an expression of pride. It reflects completion of a commitment and offers a revealing sense that God can work through you, and service does accomplish something in us and for others.

In order to find projects which the group can do, a group should develop a list of needs around them in the church, the neighborhood, the community, the country, and the world. Developing a possible project list is not manufacturing service projects but becoming aware of real needs. And there are real needs all around us. As the group makes a list, they will discover some projects they cannot do. Others they may be able to do may not be as glamorous. The very act of choosing a project which they feel needs to be done may develop a real sense of the purpose and mission of this project. Becoming aware of the potential value of the project is an important step in having it become a fulfilling experience for the group.

EVALUATION

In carrying out a project for and with others, a group should communicate to the recipients of the project that what the group is doing is aiding the group as well as the recipients. Thus, those receiving the aid of the project are involved in giving also. When the project itself is seen as a two-way experience for both parties, then we get away from the paternalistic attitude which sometimes curtails or sours a service project experience.

It is great to give. In God's economy, giving is always receiving. Capitalizing upon the interest of youth to give and guiding them into meeting real needs on both parts is a beautiful and rewarding responsibility for you as a youth worker.

THE PLAY'S THE THING – FOR LOOSENING UP, FOR GROUP-BUILDING, FOR COMMUNICATING

by LUCINDA C. RAY

Drama in youth ministry has traditionally been viewed as a vehicle for examining significant issues. This use of drama continues to be important. Drama is also helpful in loosening up a group and in building a sense of togetherness within the group.

If your church youth group is typical, its members include some who are interested, some who are indifferent, and some who are painfully self-conscious about participating in drama. The process of giving these people sheets of paper with lines for them to read or memorize may not result in the production for which you had hoped. Before your group members plunge into the structure of a specific play or role-playing situation, they may need loosening up and freeing up.

Theater games are group exercises which are remarkable in their ability to loosen and free people, as individuals and as a group, for creative activity. A series of these exercises is suggested here. You may be able to think of others. However, the general progression from simple to more involved is important to follow.

THEATER GAMES

LOOSENING UP AND BODY AWARENESS (10 minutes)

Rationale

Most people are self-conscious and tense if asked to perform, but they are frequently powerless to locate or relax this tension.

Exercise

1. Have everyone lie on the floor. Tell them that they all have wonderful, useful, fancy bodies, but much energy is expended when they are nervous. Help them experience relaxation in contrast with tension.

2. Ask the participants to tighten up every muscle in their bodies: fingers, ankles, stomach, throat, calves, ears. Name the parts. Keep reminding them by naming body parts.

3. After about one minute, say, "Now relax." Then point out how much work it takes to be tense.

4. Next, help them relax more specifically by asking them to tighten and then relax individual

114

muscles, beginning with toes, insteps, ankles, heels, etc. Be as specific as possible. Even teeth can be a source of tension! (Remember, concentrating tension on a specific body part, such as a tense neck, can also be a great key to creating a character in a script.)

5. After you have helped them to become aware of every muscle and have helped them to relax, gradually get them to sit up. Take this exercise slowly. Some people are completely relaxed only when they're sleeping!

6. As an extension of this exercise, try doing it standing up, or while the group walks around the room.

BODY MOVEMENT *(5 minutes)*

Rationale

Faced with a performance, many people become physically immobilized. For many the range of acceptable body movements is *very* small. Bodies can do many things that we normally don't allow them to do—think of all the fun we miss!

Exercise

1. You, the leader, can help to free the group by contorting your own body as grotesquely as possible. The more absurd *you* look, the less uncomfortable *they* will feel about their own bodies.

2. Ask the group members to move their bodies in as many different ways as they can think of. Suggest things like: putting head between legs, heel behind ear, jumping, stomping, walk holding ankles. Have everyone move at the same time, so that no one is on display. Continue for 3–5 minutes.

3. Keep reminding them that "it's OK to experiment," "give your body a holiday," "think of how bored your body usually is." The more encouragement you give, the more creative and experimental your group will become.

NOISES *(2–3 minutes)*

Rationale

Same as Body Movement.

Exercise

Point out how few noises people are allowed to make: speaking, singing, whistling, and sometimes crying or shouting. Help them by making a few weird beeps, blats, honks, rasps. Then ask everybody to experiment with noises *at the same time,*

so no one is listening to anyone else. Most groups find this exhilarating.

MACHINES *(10 minutes)*

Rationale

Let the group see that the exercises used so far can be given some meaning. Have fun.

Exercise

1. Ask each person to select one movement and one sound which he or she can repeat easily and rhythmically. (For example, flexing arms and saying Blug-Blug-Blug-Wheeeeee.)

2. Start with one person in the center doing his movement and sound. One at a time, each person then physically connects to the previous person with his own movement and sound.

3. When all are connected, it should be a moving, bobbing, noisy, humming machine. Try commanding it to speed up, slow down, or break down.

4. If your group is large enough, divide into two groups (8–10 each) so each can see the other machine. Every machine will always be different.

5. An extension of this exercise might be to try message machines: a happy machine, an angry machine, a lonely machine. Using words and sounds, try a litter machine (throwing cans and wrappers), a begging machine, an ecology machine, an advertising machine, an assembly line.

6. Your group members will be more creative in these ideas if you have given them a chance to explore a range of movement and sound first. You may need to take a break part-way through and loosen them up again.

GIVING FACES *(5–10 minutes)*

Rationale

This exercise is like Noises and Movement, except it increases contact between members of the group.

Exercise

1. Ask the group to sit on the floor in a tight circle.

2. The leader starts, explaining that he or she will "give" a face to the next person. That person will try to duplicate the face until the giver is satisfied. Then the "mirror" modifies the face into a new one and gives that new face to the next person.

3. Make the original face as weird as possible, so that people will be willing to try anything.

4. Go around the circle several times.

5. As an extension of this exercise, you might want to try having the first person *mold* the second person's face with his hands, like clay, creating a new face. The person whose face has been molded finds out what he or she looks like by having the third person mirror the face with his own. The second person then molds the third person's face, and so on. [Warning, some people may find the molding too threatening.]

GIVING MOVEMENT AND SOUND *(10 minutes)*

Rationale

Same as faces.

Exercise

1. Group should form large circle, standing.

2. Leader stands in the center and then creates a movement and sound—perhaps squatting, quacking like a duck, and flapping wings.

3. The leader waddles up to someone in the circle. The chosen person moves into the circle with the leader, duplicating the leader's movement and sound. When the leader is satisfied, he moves out.

4. The new leader then modifies the duck routine into something of his own choice, picks someone else, and the game continues.

MASKS *(10–15 minutes)*

Rationale

To help group members create dialogue and character in a non-threatening way.

Advance Preparation Needed)

Exercise

1. Provide the group with cut-out face masks made from poster board with cartoon-type faces drawn on in magic marker: old people, children, villains, hippies, beauty queens, football players, animals—anything which suggests a character.

2. Each group member selects a mask and creates a voice and body position for the character.

3. Pair up the people and give everyone the same simple conflict situation (i.e., one tries to beg money from the other; one person in a hurry to buy something while the other is taking his time selling; one person sitting in a seat assigned to the other at a play or sporting event, etc.).

4. The pairs hold a dialogue for 1–2 minutes. Then ask everyone to switch partners. Continue four or five times. Since the whole group is talking at once, there is no audience. Remind the group to let the created character do the talking.

These exercises should help your group members become more comfortable with each other and with their own capabilities to create. (In fact, they may be helpful exercises to warm up for any type of program.) I frequently end such a program by handing out copies of James Thurber's *The Last Flower* (or "The Owl Who Was God," "The Unicorn in the Garden") and let the whole group act out the story while one member reads it. Again, no one is responsible for memorizing lines, and all can be free to move and interpret the story.

Parables from the New Testament; readings from the Old Testament such as Job, Psalms, or Proverbs; poetry; news stories from newspapers or magazines would also be effective. This is your chance as a leader to direct their creative energy toward an issue or idea.

Here are some of Jesus' Parables which make good drama material:

	Matthew
Pearl of great price	13:45-46
Unforgiving servant	18:21-35
Wicked husbandmen in vineyard	21:33-41
Guests declining an invitation to a feast	22:1-14
Strain gnat: swallow camel	23:24
Ten virgins	25:1-13
Sheep and goats	25:31-46

	Luke
Two debtors	7:40-49
Good Samaritan	10:25-37
Friend at midnight	11:5-13
Prodigal son	15:11-24
Elder brother	15:25-32
Rich man and Lazarus	16:19-31
Two prayers	18:9-14

Following a session using Theater Games, your group may move comfortably into role playing, simulation games, play reading, or even play production. But don't forget that the whole concept of exploration of the body as a way of communication, and of assuming another character as demanded by role playing or play production, is really a very difficult process. Adolescents are already unsure of who they are, and adults may have a great deal invested in maintaining their self-image. It may be well to use exercises such as these frequently for warm-up exercises before going on to a script or role.

116

VALUES OF DRAMA

A major benefit which drama can offer to your youth group is involvement and group-building. If you can get them turned on to a script and involved in rehearsals and preparations like costumes, scenery, publicity, lighting, props, you will have a ready-made series of programs, regularly attended by a committed, enthusiastic group of youth. You will learn about and from each other, rely on each other, and become a cohesive group in a way not often experienced in a Sunday evening program series. What is more, you may end up with a production which will help others in your church and community "see what the young people are up to."

CHOOSING PLAYS

A word here about choice of material is in order. Much of what is available in play catalogues under the heading "religious drama" is poor material. Use a good play which has something important to say and then help the group to identify the relationships between the play and their understanding of the Christian faith. After all, the aesthetic taste of today's young people is highly refined, due to the mass media, and material written only for use in churches is not likely to meet the standards we use even in TV viewing. Below are some suggestions for material.

If you're a novice director, start with easy material and work up. A short one-act play, done well and enjoyed by all, is a far better experience than a long, agonizing, poorly-done classic.

An excellent comprehensive resource for the beginner is *Drama Resource*: Resources for Youth Ministry; Volume 2, Number 1, Winter 1970; The Lutheran Church Missouri Synod. (Check to see if this is available in your nearest religious bookstore.)

Most of the plays listed below can be located in your local community or school library. Those marked with a star are available in religious bookstores.

ONE-ACT PLAYS	Cast Size	Issues
Two in a Trap by Arlene Hale*	2 women	poverty/wealth
Hello Out There by William Saroyan	2 men, 1 woman	self-discovery
Wandering by Sanford Wilson	2 men, 1 woman	adolescent looks at life
Infancy by Thornton Wilder	3 men, 2 women	education
Aria da Capo by Edna St. Vincent Millay	4	war and peace
Santa Claus by e.e. cummings	10+	giving
Impromptu by Tad Mosel	2 men, 2 women	communication
Dino by Reginald Rose	10+	juvenile delinquency
Spoon River Anthology by E. L. Masters	any number	people
Three New Dramatic Works and 19 Other Very Short Plays by William Saroyan	any number	short sketches on many subjects

LONGER PLAYS		
Inherit the Wind by Lawrence and Lee	40+	truth (Scopes trial)
J. B. by Archibald MacLeish	20+	based on book of Job
For Heaven's Sake by Kromer and Silver*	10	musical satire on the church
Godspell by Stephen Schwartz	10	musical review based on book of Matthew

ADDITIONAL RESOURCES FOR THE DIRECTOR

The Stage Manager's Handbook by Bert Gruver
(New York: The Drama Book Shop, 1953)

Playmaking with Children from Kindergarten Through Junior High School by Winifred Ward
(New York: Appleton-Century-Crofts, 1957)

RESOURCES

All three volumes of *Respond* contain different listings of resources. If the resource you are looking for is not listed here, try *Respond, Volume 1* or *2*.

No attempt is made to evaluate the resources, but brief descriptions give pertinent information about subject matter, type of media, price, source.

When possible, resources should be previewed before purchasing to determine if they are appropriate for your group.

SYMBOLS

B: Book
F: Film
FS: Filmstrip
MM: Mixed Media
P: Picture or Photo
Ph: Pamphlet
R: Record
SG: Simulation Game
T: Tape

STUDY/ACTION RESOURCES

THE BIBLE

Gospel Game (SG)
Simulates the writing of contemporary gospels of the New Testament under the conditions of New Testament times. Order from: John Washburn, P.O. Box 6855, Santa Rosa, CA 95406. $3.00.

The Last Times (SG)
This game allows you to experience first-century Palestine. The focus is on political and religious events which climax in Passion Week. Rental, $5.00; Sale $10.00. Order from Brite Games, Box 371, Moline, IL 61265.

People Are Talking (R)
Jesus spots originally prepared for radio broadcast. (Available for in-church use only.) Rental $1.00 from: Librarian, Division of Mass Media, The Board of National Missions of the United Presbyterian Church in the U.S.A., Rm. 1901, 475 Riverside Drive, New York, NY 10027.

Simulation Exercises on the Sayings of Jesus (SG)
Experiential activities which help students get "inside" the parables and teachings of Jesus. Order from: John Washburn, P.O. Box 6855, Santa Rosa, CA 95406. $5.00.

Using Biblical Simulations (B)
By Donald Miller, Graydon Snyder, and Robert Neff. Tells how to use simulation and role play to study the Bible. Judson Press. $4.95.

CAREER GUIDANCE

Church Vocations—A New Look (B)
By Murray J. S. Ford. Describes a wide variety of occupations related in some way to the church. Judson Press. $2.50.

First Things First (FS)
Demonstrates the importance of making a vocational decision early in life with a clear Christian motivation or a goal in mind. For junior high up. 80-frame filmstrip, color. Leader's Guide and Reading Record. Order from: Abingdon Audiographics, Nashville, TN 37202.

Life Careers (SG)
A simulation of certain features of the labor market, the education market, and the marriage market. Rental $4.50 from: Simulation, Church Center for the United Nations, 777 United Nations Plaza, Room 10E, New York, NY 10017.

Listen, Listen (F)

Each man must do his own choosing about his life's work and then act accordingly. Order from: Educational Affairs Department, Ford Motor Company, American Road, Dearborn, MI. Free.

CHRISTIAN FAITH AND PERSONAL GROWTH

An Andrew Webber and Tim Rice Interview (T)

A 60-minute cassette tape on which the authors of *Jesus Christ Superstar* discuss how they put the show together, their own views, etc. Discussion guide included. Order from Lutheran Church Supply Store, 2900 Queen Lane, Philadelphia, PA 19129. $5.95.

Is It Always Right to Be Right? (F)

A parable in which a country reaches a crisis because, when differences arose among the people, each side stood firm in its rightness. Animated cartoon; winner of Academy Award for best animated short subject. 16mm film; color; 8 min. Rental $25.00 from: Steven Bosustow Productions, 20548 Pacific Coast Highway, Malibu, CA 90265.

For Man's Sake (B)

By John Faulstich. A 64-page booklet described as a "do-it-yourself" book on theology for high-school-age and older youth. United Church Press. 50¢ at religious bookstores.

The Lesson (R)

A modern parable, originally prepared for radio broadcast. (Available for in-church use only.) Rental $1.00 from: Librarian, Division of Mass Media/The Board of National Missions of the United Presbyterian Church in the U.S.A., Rm. 1901, 475 Riverside Dr., New York, NY 10027.

Let Faith Be Your Camera (MM)

By Wilbur Patterson. Flip chart, 11″ x 17″, designed to illustrate the idea that "faith to the Christian is a continuing dialogue between being and doing." $2.50.

The Doodle Film (F)

The story of a compulsive doodler. Illustrates growing trend away from conformity. 16mm, color, 10 min. Rental $15.00 from Learning Corporation of America, 711 Fifth Ave., New York, NY 10022.

Normal Adolescence (B)

Group for the Advancement of Psychiatry offers insights and helpful information on adolescence. Order from: Family Life Publications, P.O. Box 427, Saluda, NC 28773. $1.65.

Raw Love (RAP 5) (T)

Part of the RAP tape series by Dennis Benson. A six-session study on "the hard, cold truth about a little-understood fact of life." Published by Abingdon Press. Available at religious bookstores. $7.95.

Science and Faith—Twin Mysteries (B)

By William G. Pollard. The Christian looks at similarities and differences in science and faith. Part of the Youth Forum series. Thomas Nelson Inc. $1.95.

Tension (RAP 1) (T)

Part of the RAP tape series by Dennis Benson. Guides a group in understanding and dealing with tension. Published by Abingdon Press. Available in religious bookstores. $7.95.

A Time to Seek (B)

By Lee Fisher. Deals with the issues of life and faith which confront young people today. Abingdon Press. $1.95.

Up the Establishment (RAP 6) (T)
Part of the RAP tape series by Dennis Benson. Subtitled "How to Sell the Body for the Daily Bread While Keeping the Soul Pure and Unmortgaged." Abingdon Press. $7.95 at religious bookstores.

The Value Game (SG)
Helps groups understand how values change and are changed by events and situations. People try to make honest decisions as they judge the actions of others. 10-20 situations occur. 5-35 people. Time: 1-2 hours. Herder & Herder. $7.95 at religious bookstores.

What Makes Service Christian (B)
By Boyd Nelson. Christ came to us in service that we might learn from his example. Biblical values remind followers of Christ that their vocation is of necessity one of service. Friendship Press. 65¢ at religious bookstores.

Why Man Creates (F)
The many aspects of human creativity are well thought-out in this excellent production. Color. 25 minutes. Free from Modern Talking Pictures, 1212 Avenue of the Americas, New York, NY 10036.

Youth Considers Doubt and Frustration (B)
By Paul Holmer. Helps youth deal with adolescent doubts and frustrations. Thomas Nelson Inc. $1.50 at religious bookstores.

Youth Considers Personal Moods (B)
By Reuel Howe. Helps youth understand and deal with the "moods" they experience during adolescence. Thomas Nelson Inc. $1.95 at religious bookstores.

Youth—Where the Action Is (B)
A Through-the-Week resource for youth which relates home and school issues, such as science, history, and problems facing the nation and world. Cooperative Press. Leader's Guide, $3.45; Student's Book, $1.75 at religious bookstores.

COMMUNICATION

Communicating with Junior Highs (B)
By Robert Browning. How to listen to, learn from, and engage in dialogue with younger teens. Abingdon Press. $1.95 at religious bookstores.

Generation Gap (SG)
The game simulates the interaction between a youth and his parent. Certain issues are set up which must be reconciled. Conflict is present. Parents and teens do not compete against each other but against other teens and parents playing the game. 4-10 players. ½-1 hour. Western Publishing Co., Inc. $15.00 at religious bookstores.

High Wall? Low Wall? No Wall? (B)
By Ruth Cheney. A look at the walls that separate parts of our lives; between friends; youth and their parents; black and white; rich and poor. Especially for junior highs. Friendship Press. $1.75 at religious bookstores.

Parent-Adolescent Communication Inventory, Form A (Ph)
Assessment of parent-teen relations for both counseling and teaching. Provides clues to communication difficulties, promotes understanding. Order from Family Life Publications, Inc., Box 427, Saluda, NC 28773. Specimen set, 35¢.

Youth Considers Parents as People (B)
By Randolph C. Miller. Attacks the communication gap between parents and youth. Thomas Nelson Inc. $1.50 at religious bookstores.

DRUGS, ALCOHOL, SMOKING

Barney Butt (F)
Animated film cartoon dealing with smoking and the heart. 16mm, color, 12 min. Contact your local Heart Association for rental.

Drugs (RAP 4) (T)
Part of the RAP tape series by Dennis Benson. Helps a group study the implications of drug abuse. Published by Abingdon Press. $7.95 at religious bookstores.

The Drug Game (F)
A short TV spot on drug abuse. 16mm, color, 60 sec. Rental $5.00 from: Librarian, Division of Mass Media/The Board of National Missions of the United Presbyterian Church in the U.S.A., Room 1901, 475 Riverside Drive, New York, NY 10027.

Family Life Filmstrips, Series I (FS)
An objective overview of vital, current health areas. For junior high up.
1. Tobacco and Your Health
2. Alcohol and Your Health
3. Venereal Disease and Your Health
4. Drug Misuse and Your Health

Each filmstrip with Teacher's Guide, $7.00. Set of four filmstrips, 2 records, 4 teacher's guides: $32.50. Order from: Family Life Publications, Inc., P.O. Box 427, Saluda, NC 28773.

The Long Trip (F)
A short TV spot on drug abuse. 16mm, color, 60 sec. Rental, $5.00 from: Librarian, Division of Mass Media/The Board of National Missions of the United Presbyterian Church in the U.S.A., Room 1901, 475 Riverside Drive, New York, NY 10027.

99 Plus Films on Drugs
Evaluation of films on drugs and drug abuse. Order from: Educational Film Library Association, 17 West 60th Street, New York, NY 10023. $3.00.

Pot Is Rot and Other Horrible Facts About Bad Things (B)
By Jean C. Vermes. Facts youth need to know about health dangers in cigarettes, alcohol, drugs, and VD. Association Press. $1.75.

Smoke (F)
A satirical film depicting the reasons people smoke. 16mm, b&w, 10 min. Rental: $6.00, from Cinema 16, 175 Lexington Avenue, New York, NY 10016.

What About Drinking? (F)
A discussion of the problems of drinking. 16mm, b&w, 10 min. Order from: The Methodist Service Department, 100 Maryland Avenue, N.E., Washington, D.C. 20002.

Young People and Drinking (B)
By Arthur H. Cain. A psychologist specializing in treating alcoholics provides information from which youth can make wise decisions for themselves. John Day Company, 1968. $3.40.

ECOLOGY

Cry of the Marsh (F)
This film documents vividly the destructive processes to wild life and natural resources when a prairie marsh is drained and burned. Color, 12 min. Rental, $14.00 from: Bill Snyder Films, Box 2784, Fargo, ND 51802.

Earthcare Packet (MM)
Packet of materials on the various aspects of Christian concern for the environment, including a book, *New Ethic for a New Earth,* leader's guide and resource pamphlets. Friendship Press. $3.95 at religious bookstores.

Ecology Probe—Planet Earth (F)
A serious environmental problem is dealt with by studying the problem through a science fiction treatment. 16mm, color, 10 min. Order from: Fordham Publishing Company, 2377 Hoffman Street, Bronx, NY 10458.

The Environment and You (B)
By Richard A. Baer, Jr. Booklet from Issue and Action Packet. Published by United Church Press. Total packet, $24.95. Booklet, 95¢ at religious bookstores.

Environmental Action: Recycling Resources
A junior high course on environmental problems and solutions. Teacher's manual, student's book, two filmstrips, record, simulation game. $12.50. Order from: Office of Environmental Affairs, Continental Can Company, 633 Third Avenue, New York, NY 10017.

Population (RAP 3) (T)
Part of the RAP tape series by Dennis Benson. Helps a group study the problems of the environment. Published by Abingdon Press. $7.95 at religious bookstores.

INTERNATIONAL MISSION

Conflict (SG)
A game which simulates a futuristic model of a disarmed world based on a nation-state system. Designed to enable learners to consider imaginative alternative structures for the future. For 24-36 players. Rental, $12.50 from: Simulation, Church Center for the United Nations, 777 United Nations Plaza, Room 10E, New York, NY 10017.

Crisis (SG)
Participants become members of six nations and try to resolve a tense situation in a mining area of enormous importance to the entire world. For 18-

36 players. Order from: Western Behavioral Sciences Institute, P.O. Box 1023, La Jolla, CA 92037. $25.00.

The Cross Is Lifted (B)
By Chandran Devanesen. A small volume of poems about India and her people, planned for personal or group use. Sensitive drawings by Frank Wesley illustrate the book, expressing the truths of the Christian faith through the symbols of Indian Art. Friendship Press. $1.25 at religious bookstores.

Mandate for Mission (B)
By Eugene L. Smith. The big, complex world is all around us. What does this constantly changing situation mean to the church? Friendship Press. $1.75 at religious bookstores.

Dangerous Parallel (SG)
A simulation of international negotiation and decision-making in which the participants are divided into six teams representing the cabinets of six nations involved in a world crisis. For 18-36 players. Rental $7.50 from: Simulation, Church Center for the United Nations, 777 United Nations Plaza, Room 10E, New York, NY 10017. Sale $60.00 from Scott Foresman and Company, 1900 East Lake Avenue, Glenview, IL 60025.

End of the Dialogue (F)
A documentary study of apartheid in South Africa. The harsh reality of enforced racial separation and oppression of black Africans by a small white minority is portrayed. Housing, employment, education, recreation, and police surveillance are some of the areas covered. Color, 42 min. Cokesbury. Rental, $15.00 from Mass Media Associates, 2116 North Charles Street, Baltimore, MD 21218.

Fun and Festival from India, Pakistan, Ceylon and Nepal (B)
By Irene Wells and Jean Bothwell. An updating of

this perennial favorite. Contains games, recipes, songs, readings, dress, and many program ideas. A useful book for all ages, both in groups and for solo reading. Friendship Press. 95¢ at religious bookstores.

Future-Maker in India: The Story of Sarah Chakko (B)
By Mary Louise Slater. A gifted teacher gave her students a great legacy: her ideal of poise as a sense of proportion, of appreciation of relative values, both material and spiritual. Miss Chakko, a born leader, was a president of the World Council of Churches. Friendship Press. 95¢ at religious bookstores.

Journey into Nigeria (F)
A film giving a well-rounded view of life in one of the newly independent countries. Presents the situation of the Christian church there and attitude of the church toward missionaries. Color, 35 min. Cokesbury. Rental, $10.00 from Mass Media Associates, 2116 North Charles Street, Baltimore, MD 21218.

Mission with Integrity in India (B)
By Renuka Mukerji Somasekhar. Equally at home in India and the West, the author speaks the truth in love about both churches and mission boards and about their often uneasy relationships in these days of change. She has extensive experience within the Indian church. Friendship Press. $1.25 at religious bookstores.

Sing the Glory of Africa (FS)
The glories of Africa, past and present, are celebrated in this full-color filmstrip. Side 1 of recording contains narrative of script. Side 2 includes music and folktales from Africa. Color. 33⅓ rpm record. Sale, $10.00 from: The Service Center, 7820 Reading Road, Cincinnati, OH 45237.

Tauw (F)
A typical day in the life of a 20-year-old African man points up problems of social change; the generation gap, the breakdown of family life. Filmed in Dakar by the Senegalese producer Ousmane Sambene, whose sensitive work has won him world recognition. Color, 26 minutes. Cokesbury. Rental, $12.00 from Mass Media Associates, or your local film depository.

Walk the Distant Hills: The Story of Longri Ao (B)
By Richard G. Beers. This Christian leader of India played a reconciling role when India was being separated from British rule and had to cope with tribal divisiveness. As a strong man of peace, he walked the Naga hills in behalf of unity. Friendship Press. 95¢ at religious bookstores.

JUSTICE AND CIVIL LIBERTIES

Confronted! (B)
By Myra Scovel, et al. Discussion Starters on Faith and Justice and on India. Walk-on dramas requiring no props or memorization of parts. Groups will find many hours of good discussion flowing from the use of these brief dramas. Friendship Press. $1.35 at religious bookstores.

Don't Church Me In (R)
By Allan E. Sloane. The old struggle between the established church and its newer, more aggressive leaders is dramatized in a witty yet provocative manner. Recording 33⅓ rpm. Friendship Press. $5.00 at religious bookstores.

Get out There and Do Something About Injustice (B)
By Margaret E. Kuhn. A study-action manual to work toward doing faith and having justice. Friendship Press. $1.95 at religious bookstores.

Guide on "Faith and Justice" for Adult and Youth Groups (B)
By Wayne Bryan. Bright, creative, fresh ways of using study materials on Faith and Justice. Friendship Press. $1.25 at religious bookstores.

Good News, Anyone? (B)
By Jean Louise Smith. A group process book helps junior and middle highs analyze ways in which contemporary artists, musicians, and writers may be helping us relate the tenets of the Christian faith to the injustices in modern society. Friendship Press. $2.75 at religious bookstores.

Grace at Point Zero (B)
By Loren E. Halvorson. Writing in the form of an imaginary script of the future, the author takes a hard look at what he calls "an unhealthy separation of Christian faith and social justice." Friendship Press. $1.75 at religious bookstores.

Handbook of Everyday Law (B)
By Martin J. Ross. A home legal encyclopedia which is easy to understand. Harper & Row, Publishers. 95¢ at most bookstores.

Look Back and Dream: Great Moments in Mission (R)
By Warren Mild. Dramatic episodes in the lives of Christians of other generations who sought to relate faith and justice in meaningful ways. Included are Walter Rauschenbusch, early exponent of Christian social action; Dorothea Dix, who campaigned energetically for reform in mental hospitals; William Carey, Robert Raikes. 33⅓ rpm record. Friendship Press. $5.00 at religious bookstores.

See It! Do It! Your Faith in Action (B)
By David Ng. Yes, you *can* do something about injustice—and here is a book to help young people see it and then act to correct it. You will walk through ancient Bethel with the prophet Amos and visit modern Chinatown, San Francisco. You can discover social justice in the arts, learn how to start an underground newspaper, work at renovating a town. And finally, with the help of a list of possibilities, you can plan actions to promote justice in your own town. Friendship Press. $2.50 at religious bookstores.

To Set Things Right: The Bible Speaks on Faith and Justice (B)
By Justin Vander Kolk. Is today's demand among Christians for greater concern for social justice scriptural? Yes, by all means, says the author as he probes the deep biblical roots of the demand for social justice. Here is a Bible study piece for individual or group use that will undergird our understanding of the whole thrust of the "Faith and Justice" issue. Friendship Press. $1.25 at religious bookstores.

Up Against the Law: The Legal Rights of People Under 21 (B)
By Jean Strouse. Explanation of laws which are particularly relevant to youth, in such areas as: students' rights, marriage, drugs, sex, driving, the draft. New American Library Inc. 95¢ at religious bookstores.

Voices of Protest and Hope (B)
Compiled by Elisabeth D. Dodds. The world, through contemporary writers, speaks to the church in no uncertain terms about justice as they see it and seek it. Friendship Press. $1.95 at religious bookstores.

NATIONAL MISSION

Change (RAP 2) (T)
Part of the RAP tape series by Dennis Benson. Helps a group deal with change in society. Published by Abingdon Press. $7.95 at religious bookstores.

127

The Church Resources Game (SG)
A simulation about the mission of the church: what that mission should be, what resources are required, and how existing resources can best be used. The game forces the players to think about mission in the concrete terms of resources and situations. Cost: $9.95. Available for purchase directly from Urbandyne, 5659 S. Woodlawn Ave., Chicago, IL 60637 or Urbandyne, P.O. Box 741, Saratoga, CA 95070.

PEACE

The Draft—Decisions, Issues, Actions
By Russell G. Claussen. Booklet from Issues and Action Packet. Published by United Church of Christ. Packet, $24.95. Booklet, 95¢ at religious bookstores.

Hiroshima & Nagasaki (F)
Filmed by Japanese photographers immediately after the bombings, this is by far the most poignant statement of the horror of nuclear war ever produced. 16mm, b&w; 15 min. Rental, $15.00 from SANE, 1307 Sansom Street, Philadelphia, PA 19107. *Rental within 24-hour bus service of Philadelphia only.*

Interviews with My-Lai Veterans (F)
1971 Academy Award winner for best documentary short. Interview with five American soldiers who were at My-Lai are compressed into a candid recollection. 16mm, color; 22 min. Rental $25.00 from SANE, 1307 Sansom Street, Philadelphia, PA 19107. *Rental within 24-hour bus service of Philadelphia only.*

POVERTY

The Food Crisis (F)
Areas of the world in which starvation is a way of

life are contrasted with those of abundance. 16mm, b&w; 60 min. Rental $10.00 from: Mass Media Ministries, 2116 North Charles Street, Baltimore, MD 21218.

Hunger and Poverty (B)
By Tilford E. Dudley. Booklet from Issues and Action Packet. Published by United Church of Christ. Packet, $24.95. Booklet, 95¢ at religious bookstores.

If I Were You (B)
By Barbara Smith. A group project book for early teens to stimulate a deeper awareness of the injustices poverty often inflicts on its powerless victims. Friendship Press. $1.75 at religious bookstores.

Liberate the Captives (FS)
Shows how people of low economic status in a community can be brought together and organized to start working toward solutions of their own problems. Color filmstrip. Filmstrip with script $7.50. Filmstrip with record $10.00. Available at religious bookstores.

Starpower (SG)
Players assume roles as members of groups in a class society. Identifies abuses of power, characteristics of social organization, and communication skills. For 20-40 players. Complete kit, rental, $3.00 from: Simulation, Church Center for the United Nations, 777 United Nations Plaza, Room 10E, New York, NY 10017. Sale: instructions only, $3.00; complete kit, $35.00 from: Western Behavioral Sciences Institute, P.O. Box 1023, La Jolla, CA 92037.

Whenever People Hurt (FS)
The problem of hunger through the eyes of American youth. Sale, $3.50 from: National Council of Churches, 475 Riverside Drive, New York, NY 10027.

POWER

Disarmament (SG)

A simulation which involves two groups in the problems of conflict, trust, and negotiation. For 8-30 players. Instructions and discussion guide available from: Simulation, Church Center for the United Nations, 777 United Nations Plaza, Room 10E, New York, NY 10017.

Napoli (SG)

A simulation in which the participants serve as members of a legislature and attempt to be re-elected at the end of a term. Valuable ethical reflection may come from considering the sources and power of influences on their election. For about 40 players. Rental, $4.50 from: Simulation, Church Center for the United Nations, 777 United Nations Plaza, Room 10E, New York, NY 10017.

The Money Game (SG)

Simulates some of the economic interactions between developed (rich) and developing (poor) nations. For 18 players. 25¢ per copy. Order from Concern magazine, 475 Riverside Drive, Room 401, New York, NY 10027.

Plans (SG)

Participants are members of interest groups using their influence to produce change in American society. For 12-36 players. Rental, $4.50 from: Simulation, Church Center for the United Nations, 777 United Nations Plaza, Room 10E, New York, 10017.

Politics Is People (MM)

A study unit for junior highs which deals with political responsibility and encourages action. $3.50. Order from: Christian Board of Publication, Box 179, St. Louis, MO 63166.

Powerplay (SG)

Five teams begin with equal amounts of power.

As they interact, the power is redistributed unevenly. For 20-50 players. Instructions available from: Simulation, Church Center for the United Nations, 777 United Nations Plaza, Room 10E, New York, NY 10017.

The Road Game (SG)

A study of competition. Teams (red, blue, green, yellow) attempt to build roads across each other's areas. Permission must be negotiated. Team with most roads wins. 8-35 people. Can be used with youth, children, adults. Time: 45 minutes to two hours. Herder & Herder. $7.95 at religious bookstores.

RACE RELATIONS

A Bibliography of Negro History and Culture for Young Readers (B)

By Miles M. Jackson Jr. Where to find materials on Negro history. University of Pittsburgh Press. $2.50 at most bookstores.

Black-American History and Culture (R)

A "stereo history" of black America. Order from: Scholastic Records, 906 Sylvan Avenue, Englewood Cliffs, NJ 07632.

Black Resources Center (MM)

For information about current black resources, contact: Black Resources Center, Department of Educational Development, Division of Christian Education, National Council of Churches, 475 Riverside Drive, Room 720, New York, NY 10027.

Bury My Heart at Wounded Knee (B)

By Dee Brown. Describes the "plunder" of American Indians by the white man during the second half of the nineteenth century. Holt, Rinehart & Winston. $10.95 at most bookstores.

Christian Beliefs and Anti-Semitism (B)
By Charles Y. Glock and Rodney Stark. Asks:
"Does the Christian faith currently have any effect
on attitudes toward Jews?" Harper & Row, Publishers. $1.95 at religious bookstores.

The Ebony Book of Black Achievement (B)
By Margaret Peters. A resource for black history.
Gives biographies of outstanding black men and
women. Johnson Publishing Company. $4.95 at
religious bookstores.

*Freedomways, A Quarterly Review of the Freedom
Movement* (P)
Freedomways Associates, Inc., 799 Broadway, NY
10003. $3.50 a year.

The Jesus Bag (B)
By William H. Grier and Price M. Cobbs. Case
histories and commentary on the black experience
in religion. McGraw-Hill. $6.95 at most book-
stores.

Let's Face Racism (B)
By Nathan Wright, Jr. The Christian looks at
racism. Part of the Youth Forum Series. Thomas
Nelson Inc. $1.95 at religious bookstores.

Life and Times of Frederick Douglass (B)
Edited by Genevieve S. Gray. Biography of the
runaway slave who became an advisor to Abraham
Lincoln. Grossett & Dunlap. $4.50 at most book-
stores.

The Mechanical Man (F)
A short TV spot on race relations. 16mm, color.
30 sec. Rental $5.00 from: Librarian, Division of
Mass Media, The Board of National Missions of
the United Presbyterian Church in the U.S.A.,
Room 1901, 475 Riverside Drive, New York,
NY 10027.

The Negro in America, A Bibliography (B)
Compiled by Elizabeth W. Miller and Mary L.

Fisher. Cambridge, MA: Harvard University Press.
$10.00 at most bookstores.

Today's Negro Voices by Beatrice M. Murphy (B)
Poems of black youth from 13 to 20. Simon and
Schuster. $2.95 at most bookstores.

We Will Suffer and Die If We Have To (D)
By Colin Hodgetts. A folk play about the polar-
ization of blacks torn between the nonviolent and
violent movements. Judson Press. $1.95 at re-
ligious bookstores.

Sex and Family Life

Between Parent and Teenager (B)
By Haim G. Ginott. Specific communication advice, constructively given. The Macmillan Company. $5.95 at most bookstores.

Christian View of Sex Education (B)
By Martin F. Wessler. Opportunities for sex education by pastors, teachers, youth workers. Offers
approaches and programs. Concordia. $2.25 at
religious bookstores.

Dating Problems Checklist (Ph)
Enables high school and college students to register
their problems and talk freely with counselors and
group leaders. Order from: Family Life Publications, Inc., Box 427, Saluda, NC 28773. Specimen
set 35¢.

Facts About Sex (B)
By Sol Gordon. A first book about sex for young
people who do not like to read but want to know.
John Day. $3.95; paper, $1.90 at most bookstores.

Facts You Should Know About VD (B)
By Andre Blanzaco, et al. Gives young people
information they should have. Lothrop, Lee and
Shepherd. $3.95 at most bookstores.

Family Life Filmstrips, Series 2 (FS)
Deals with problems faced by youth and attempts to instill a healthy respect for the consequences of undisciplined reaction and experimentation. Titles:
Running Away
Venereal Disease
Unplanned Parenthood
Suicide
Order from: Family Life Publications, Inc., P.O. Box 427, Saluda, NC 28773. Each filmstrip with teacher's guide: $8.00. Set of four filmstrips, 2 records, 4 guides: $38.00.

The First Nine Months of Life (B)
By Geraldine Flanagan. Development of a baby from fertilized egg to birth. Illustrated and detailed. Simon and Schuster. $4.95 at most bookstores.

The Human Reproductive System (B)
By Morris Krieger and Alan Guttmacher. Details and explains human reproduction in simple language. Thoroughly illustrated. Basic biology in color. Sterling Publishing Co. $4.95 at most bookstores.

Life Can Be Sexual (B)
By Elmer N. Witt. Shows how sex, sexuality, and Christianity interrelate. For ages 15 and over. Concordia Publishing Co. $2.25 at religious bookstores.

Lucy (F)
The story of an unwed, pregnant teenager in a Puerto Rican family. Unusual insight into the feelings of the girl, her boyfriend, her family. 16mm, color, 13 min. Order from: Pictura Films Distribution Corp., 43 W. 16th Street, New York, NY 10011. Rental, $25.00.

Male/Female (B)
Contains leader's guidance and student's material

for junior high course in sex education. The Seabury Press, Inc. $1.75 at religious bookstores.

Resource Guide in Sex Education for the Mentally Retarded (B)
Resources for specialized instruction in sex education. Order from SIECUS Publications Office, 1855 Broadway, New York, NY 10023. $2.00.

Sex Before Twenty (B)
By Helen Southard. Help in making constructive decisions about dating and sex behavior for junior high and above. J. P. Dutton. $3.50 at most bookstores.

Sex Knowledge Inventory—Form Y (Ph)
Explores information and misinformation about sexuality. A good opener for a sex education program, if used wisely. Order from: Family Life Publications, Inc., Box 427, Saluda, NC 28773. Specimen set 35¢.

SIECUS Study Guides (B)
Study guides for various aspects of sex education and family life education:

#G01   Sex Education
#G02   Homosexuality
#G03   Masturbation
#G04   Characteristics of Male and Female Sexual Responses
#G05   Premarital Sexual Standards
#G11   Sexual Encounters Between Adults and Children
#G13   Concerns of Parents about Sex Education
#G14   Teenage Pregnancy: Prevention and Treatment

Order from: SIECUS Publications Office, 1855 Broadway, New York, NY 10023. 50¢ each.

Teenage Sex Counselor (B)
A book for youth reluctant to seek or receive per-

son to person guidance. Sympathetic, warmly human help for directing all aspects of maturing toward a well-adjusted adulthood. Barron's Educational Series. $1.50 at most bookstores.

To Be a Woman (F)
A film showing girls and young women speaking for themselves, about their attitudes, self-images, and their basic convictions. Discussion oriented. 16mm, color; 13 min. Order from Billy Budd Films, Inc., 235 E. 57th St., Room 8D, New York, NY 10022. Rental, $17.50.

Understanding Sex (B)
By Alan F. Guttmacher. A frank and common-sense book mainly for youth but also of great help to teachers, counselors, and parents. New American Library. $4.95 at most bookstores.

When You Marry (B)
By Evelyn Duvall and Reuben Hill. A most constructive book for older teens with serious thoughts about marriage. Association Press. $5.95 at most bookstores.

Why Wait Till Marriage (B)
By Evelyn Mills Duvall. A book to help youth understand the reasons for sexual moral standards. Association Press. 75¢ (paper) at most bookstores.

Your Dating Days (B)
By Paul Landis. Helps youth understand the opposite sex, decide when to marry, and know how to select a mate. McGraw-Hill. $3.25 at most bookstores.

Youth Considers Marriage (B)
By David R. Mace. Helps youth look at the problems and fulfillments of marriage. Part of the Youth Forum series. Thomas Nelson Inc. $1.50 at religious bookstores.

WORSHIP/CELEBRATION

Alleluia (B)
Songbook for inner-city parishes. From Cooperative Recreation Service, Inc., Delaware, OH 43105.

Banners and Such (B)
A creative approach to banner-making, written from actual workshop experiences. $4.00. Order from: Center for Contemporary Celebration, 1400 East 53rd Street, Chicago, IL 60615.

Buttons
Three original designs on buttons which can be passed out during celebrations:
1. Ankh: life symbol
2. Whole Earth—Whole People
3. Let Us Live
35¢ each. Order from: Center for Contemporary Celebration, 1400 East 53rd Street, Chicago, IL 60615.

Celebrate Life (R)
A youth-oriented record with "journey kit" (booklet which contains song lyrics and line drawings). Songs by Paul Hansen. Cover unfolds to make a 12" x 24" poster. Order from: Youth Ministry, 2900 Queen Lane, Philadelphia, PA 19129. $6.50.

Celebration for Modern Man (R)
A new concept in acoustical liturgy recorded by the Dukes of Kent jazz ensemble and the Voices of Celebration. $5.25 at religious bookstores.

Celebration Now (F)
The words and music for three contemporary Christian songs provide an audio "backdrop" for scenes of Christian acceptance. 16mm, color, 12 min.; produced by Family Films. Rental $14.00 from religious film libraries.

Change (MM)

A multimedia presentation with three reels of film (two are silent) to be run simultaneously on three 16mm film projectors and a wall large enough to project three images side by side, on three screens. Content covers the change in such areas as ecology, medicine, technology, and the concepts of God. Rental $13.00 from: Division of Mass Media, Room 1901, 475 Riverside Drive, New York, NY 10027.

Don't Turn Me Off, Lord: And Other Jailhouse Meditations (B)

By Carl F. Burke. A new collection of meditations and prayers originally prepared for use in the chapel of the jail where the author has been chaplain since 1963. Association Press. Cloth, $3.50; paper, $1.75 at religious bookstores.

The Dust and Ashes Songbook (B)

By Jim Moore and Tom Page. Songs for the Christian to use both inside and outside the church. Abingdon Press. Book, $1.50; record, $4.98 at religious bookstores.

The Holy Family (FS)

Displays and interprets nativity paintings by artists from Asia and Africa. Color filmstrip and record. Sale, $5.00 from National Council of Churches, 475 Riverside Drive, New York, NY 10027.

Hymns Hot and Carols Cool (B)

Singable tunes with words of faith. Proclamation Productions. $1.00 at religious bookstores.

Let Us Break Bread Together (B)

By Carl Staplin and Dale Miller. Guide for a contemporary communion service. Includes songs with guitar accompaniment. Bethany Press. $1.25 at religious bookstores.

Multi-Media Box (MM)

Hand-painted slides, material for making film loops, a tape of original music and sound, plus directions for creating media for use in a celebration (or in a teaching-learning experience). Order from: Synesthetics, Inc., 5933 16th St., N.W., Washington, D.C. 20011. $27.50.

Now Songs (B)

A collection of contemporary gospel songs. Abingdon Press. $2.50 at religious bookstores.

Revelation Now (F)

Three contemporary Christian songs from the well-known "Hymns for Now" collection provide a musical background for integrated visuals which show a typical nineteen- or twenty-year-old boy facing the trauma of growing up. Produced by Family Films. Rental $14.00 from religious film libraries.

Raise a Jubilee: Music in Youth Ministry (MM)

Resource for youth and adults. Discusses ways music is integrated into youth ministry. Includes two soundsheets. Published by Graded Press, Nashville, TN 37202. $4.25.

Songs for Celebration (B)

A hymnal for the church wherever it's happening! Order from: Center for Contemporary Celebration, 1400 East 53rd St., Chicago, IL 60615. $2.75.

Teaching and Celebrating Advent in Home and Church (Ph)

Packet of eight pamphlets on Advent. Order from Griggs Educational Service, 1033 Via Madrid, Livermore, CA 94550. $3.00.

Time Being (MM)

A variety of materials for preparing a celebration "happening" of up to three hours, for groups of ten to thirty. Contains weather balloons, equipment for a light show, sheet of plastic, instructions for using taste and smell in meditation, how-to instructions for celebration. Order from: John and Mary Harrell, Box 9006, Berkeley, CA 94709. $17.00.

A Time to Dance (B)
By Margaret Fisk Taylor. How to use symbolic movement or interpretive dancing in worship/celebration. United Church Press. $1.95 at religious bookstores.

Ventures in Worship (B)
A loose-leaf collection of tested models and forms of contemporary worship. Order from: Dr. D. J. Randolph, 1908 Grand Avenue, Nashville, TN 37203. $1.50.

Ventures in Worship #2 (MM)
A packet of worship materials. Abingdon Press. $2.50 at religious bookstores.

COMMUNITY MINISTRIES

God's Turf (B)
By Bob Combs. Describes the ministry of Teen Challenge to street youth and addicts. Old Tappan, NJ: Fleming H. Revell Co. $2.50 at religious bookstores.

It's Happening with Youth (B)
By Janice M. Corbett and Curtis L. Johnson. Description of youth ministries that have developed in response to community needs. Harper & Row, Publishers. $4.95 at religious bookstores.

CAMPING

Backpacking (B)
By R. C. Rethmel. Specific information on just how the backpacker keeps down the weight of his pack is the primary purpose of this book. Burgess. 95¢ at most bookstores.

Cameron Daycamp Manual (B)
A manual for training teenage-volunteer leadership for an inner-city daycamp. Order from: Griggs Educational Service, 1033 Via Madrid, Livermore, CA 94550. $3.00.

The Fun in Winter Camping (B)
How-to-do-it suggestions for winter experiences in the out-of-doors. Association Press. $1.00 at religious bookstores.

Let the Bible Speak Outdoors (B)
By Mary Elizabeth Mason. Insight, inspiration, and practical help for leaders in outdoor experiences. National Council of Churches. 70¢ at religious bookstores.

Recreation for Retarded Teenagers and Young Adults (B)
By Bernice Carlson and David R. Ginglend. Especially valuable for the camp leader. Abingdon Press. $4.95 at religious bookstores.

Try the World Out (MM)
Camping resources for early teens. Emphasizes relationships between campers and their physical environment. Leader's book, filmstrip, 2 records, student's book. Abingdon Press. $7.50 at religious bookstores.

Voices for the Wilderness (B)
Edited by William Schwartz. Leading ecology spokesmen explain their concern for the preservation of the wilderness. Ballantine. $1.25 at most bookstores.

LEADER DEVELOPMENT

Basic Bible Study for Teachers (MM)
A self-instructional filmstrip kit which trains teach-

ers to identify key persons of the Old Testament, as well as to use basic Bible reference books. Filmstrip, cassette tape recording, leader's manual, participant's worksheets. Order from: Griggs Educational Service, P.O. Box 363, Livermore, CA 94550. $12.00.

Christian Education for Socially Handicapped Children and Youth (B)
By Eleanor Ebersole. A manual for chaplains and teachers of persons under custody. United Church Press. $1.25 at religious bookstores.

Communicating the Gospel Today (MM)
A book in a box which examines the contemporary situation and describes a method for drawing theological implications. Includes directions for a workshop in non-verbal activity, art cards, sounds, incense, light. Order from John and Mary Harrell, Box 9006, Berkeley, CA 94709. $14.00.

Education and Ecstasy (B)
By G. B. Leonard. Describes a concept of learning which applies to all living things. Dell Publishing Co. $2.25 at most bookstores.

Film and Slide Making Kit (MM)
Contains everything you need for a class to create their own 16mm film and sets of slides without cameras. Order from Griggs Educational Service, 1033 Via Madrid, Livermore, CA 94550. $20.00.

40 Ways to Teach in Groups (B)
By Martha Leypoldt. A variety of group methods for learning, plus the resources to use with each method. Judson Press. $2.50 at religious bookstores.

Gaming (B)
By Dennis Benson. Helps for leaders and groups who want to create their own learning games. Includes two records which serve as resources for games described in the book. Abingdon Press. $4.95 at religious bookstores.

Growing as a Group (B)
By Robert R. Hansel. Booklet from Issues and Action Packet. United Church Press. Packet, $24.95. Booklet, 95¢ at religious bookstores.

A Handbook of Structured Experiences for Human Relations Training, Vol. III (B)
This book, plus volumes I and II, contain a wide variety of experiences that can be utilized in human relations training. Order from: University Press Associates, P.O. Box 615, Iowa City, IA 52240. $3.00.

Resources Galore (Ph)
Listings of fresh resources for creative educational ministries in the church. Order from: Gramercy Plaza, B-F, 130 East 18th Street, New York, NY 10005. $1.00.

Slide and Film Making Manual (B)
How to make slides and films without a camera. Order from: Griggs Educational Service, 1033 Via Madrid, Livermore, CA 94550. $2.00.

Teaching and Celebrating Lent—Easter (Ph)
A packet of eight pamphlets designed for teachers to use as resources in the recognition and celebration of the season of Lent and Easter. Titles: "Some Questions of Concern"; "Days to Remember and Celebrate"; "Children's Creative Writing"; "An Easter Story"; "Biblical Resources"; "Teaching Activities"; "Family Activities"; "Bibliography." Order from: Griggs Educational Service, P.O. Box 362, Livermore, CA 94550. $3.00 plus postage.

Teaching and Learning (F)
Shows actual class sessions with junior highs and discusses the methods used. 16mm, color; 22 min. Rental $12.50, from film libraries.

Teaching Early Adolescents Creatively (B)
By Edward D. Seely. A manual for church school teachers. The Westminster Press. $2.95 at religious bookstores.

Young People and Their Culture (B)
By Ross Snyder. Ways of creating a meaningful youth culture, with specific resource suggestions. Abingdon Press. $4.50 at most bookstores.

Youth, World, and Church (B)
By Sara Little. Shows how youth, who are full members of the congregation, can become involved in the church's mission. John Knox Press. $1.95 at religious bookstores.

CATALOGS

Argus Communications
Tapes, posters, books, buttons. Order from: Argus Communications, 3505 North Ashland Ave., Chicago, IL 60657.

Audio-Visual Resource Guide (B)
Over 1,800 listings of films, filmstrips, recordings, and slides, evaluated for religious education. $3.95. Order from: National Council of Churches, 475 Riverside Drive, New York, NY 10027.

Council Press Catalogue (B)
Catalog of resources available through the National Council of Churches in the area of Christian education, mission, overseas ministries, etc. Order from National Council of Churches, 475 Riverside Drive, New York, NY 10027.

A Catalog of Plays for Church Use
Order from: Baker's Plays, 100 Summer St., Boston, MA 02110.

Contemporary Drama Service
Catalog of services. Includes drama, playbits, and entertainments. Order from: Contemporary Drama Service, Box 68, Downers Grove, IL 60515.

Drug Abuse Catalog
Listing of materials related to drug abuse. $1.00. Order from: Presbyterian Distribution Service, 225 Varick Street, New York, NY 10014.

F.E.L. Church Publications
Catalog of music, recordings, and folk hymns. Order from: F.E.L. Church Publications, 22 East Huron Street, Chicago, IL 60611.

Full Circle
Interesting posters, books, films. Order from: Full Circle, 218 East 72nd Street, New York, NY 10021.

Guidance Catalog
Materials on drug education, motivational guidance, career/vocational guidance, etc. Order from: Guidance Associates of Pleasantville, NY 10570.

Guide to Educational Media (B)
By Margaret I. Rufsvold and Carolyn Guss. A list of media catalogs for films (including free films), filmstrips, kinescopes, records, tapes, programmed instruction materials, slides, public school personnel, but helpful for religious educators also. Some catalogs are free. $2.50 from American Library Association, 50 East Huron St., Chicago, IL 60611.

Kairos
Worship resources, films. Order from: Kairos, Box 24056, Minneapolis, MN 55424.

Media for Christian Formation: A Guide to Audio-Visual Resources (B)
By William A. Dalglish. Comprehensive listing of audio-visual resources that can be used in a local church. $7.50 at religious bookstores.

Reigner Recording Library Catalog
Lending library of sound recordings and sound

motion pictures, especially of well-known ministers and public speakers. Includes worship services, radio programs, television programs. Order from: Union Theological Seminary in Virginia, Richmond, VA.

PERIODICALS

Christian Art
Especially recommended for those utilizing the creative arts. Subscription $6.00. Order from: *Christian Art,* 1801 West Greenleaf Ave., Chicago, IL 60626.

Cultural Information Service
Capsulizing of the cultural scene in seven areas: Americana, Art, Drama, Film, Literature, Rock Music, Television. Subscription $6.00. Order from: Youth Ministry, 2900 Queen Lane, Philadelphia, PA 19129.

Going to College Handbook
An annual in periodical format which contains articles helpful to youth who are anticipating going to college. Order from: Outlook Publishers, 512 East Main St., Richmond, VA 23219. $1.00.

Mass Media Ministries
Bi-weekly newsletter reviewing new resources, especially films and TV programs. Subscription $10.00 per year. Order from: Mass Media Ministries, 2116 North Charles St., Baltimore, MD 21218.

Medialog
A monthly publication of the Teacher Learning Center, 1942 Virginia Street, Berkeley, CA 94709. $5.00 per ten issues.

Media Mix
Up-to-date information on films, TV, print, recordings, and other media. Subscription $5.00. Order from: George A. Pflaum, Publisher, 38 W. Fifth Street, Dayton, Ohio 45402.

Modern Media Teacher
For media people. Subscription $5.00. Order from George A. Pflaum, Publisher, 38 W. Fifth Street, Dayton, Ohio 45402.

Probe
Newsletter about new resources and creative approaches to church and community work. Subscription, $5.00 per year. Order from: *Probe,* Christian Associates of Southwest Pennsylvania, 220 Grant Street, Pittsburgh, PA 15219.

Scan
Monthly newsletter which evaluates new resources. Subscription, $6.00 from: *Scan,* P.O. Box 12811, Pittsburgh, PA 15241.

Simulation Sharing Service
An ecumenical service to provide the use of simulation gaming in the church's ministry. Subscription: $5.00 from: Simulation Sharing Service, Box 1176, Richmond, VA 23209.

Spectrum
Feature articles, media section with survey of films, filmstrips, and recordings. Subscription, $5.00. Order from: Division of Christian Education, National Council of Churches, 475 Riverside Drive, New York, NY 10027.

INDEX TO VOLUMES 1, 2, and 3 of RESPOND